IT'S ALL ABOUT HER

A Man-to-Man's Guide to Marital Bliss

HOW TO LOSE EVERY BATTLE & WIN THE WAR

JIM HAMILTON

To
Matt,
Congratulations!
I own it up!

Jim Hamilton

IT'S ALL ABOUT HER

Published by:
Library Tales Publishing, Inc.
244 5th Avenue, Suite Q222
New York, NY 10001
www.LibraryTalesPublishing.com

For general information on our other products and services, please contact our Customer Care Department at 1-800-754-5016, or fax 917-463-0892. For technical support, please visit www.LibraryTalesPublishing.com

Library Tales Publishing also publishes its books in a variety of electronic formats. Every content that appears in print is available in electronic books.

ISBN-13: 978-0615748009
ISBN-10: 0615748007

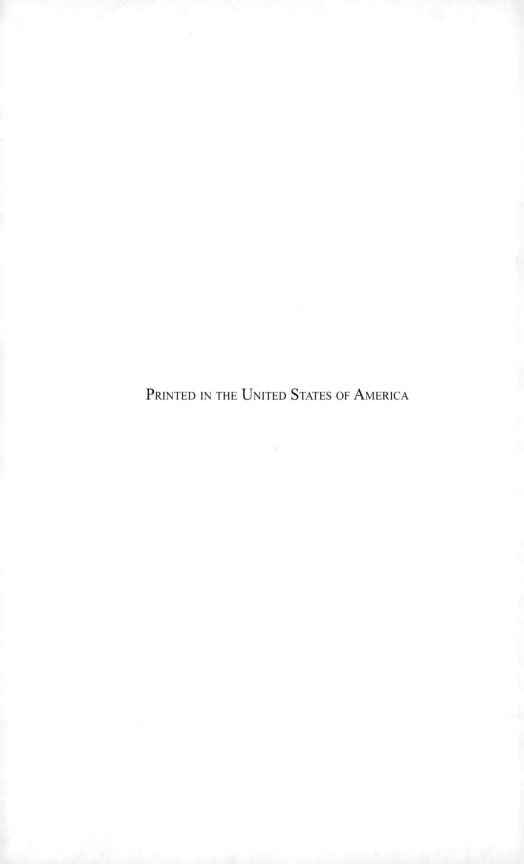

Jim Hamilton is a 50-something business consultant with over 30 years of experience in the hi-tech industry. More importantly, he is a father of three, grandfather of three, and husband to one remarkable woman. As he states in the introduction of his book: "I am not a psychologist, psychiatrist, or marital /family therapist. I am just a regular guy whose inspiration for writing this book is the love of my wife and more than a few comments from her friends that I should provide lessons to their husbands on how to do a few nice things for them once in a while. I am certainly no saint, but I can tell you that not a day goes by that I do not thank God that I am married to my wife and take a few minutes to reflect on what we have and what I can do to make it better."

A graduate of UCLA, Jim was raised in Palo Alto, CA, and currently resides in Pleasanton, CA with his extraordinary wife, Dora.

Dedicated to my Boys
Brodie, Mike, and Angelo.
May your lives and relationships be as a great
as the pride I have in calling you my sons.

Table of Contents

A Loving Truth

Care for one another each day as if it were your last.
Respect one another as if you had a million more.
Laugh with one another loudly and often,
And your Love will open Life's every door.

INTRODUCTION:

WELCOME TO THE WINNING SIDE

THE FUNDAMENTALS

*S*o you work hard. You spend 50 to 70 hours a week trying to make enough money to afford all of the essentials for your family to be comfortable. And as the definition of comfort seems to be morphing these days, to meet the needs of your family, children, educations, a little recreation, and a few toys, we are talking a lot of work...for you and your wife or partner. But you are succeeding, if not tiring.

And now you just want to have that down time...be it time in the garage to putter around; in the yard to plant that plant that will make all the difference; or in the favorite chair to read that sports magazine that makes you the expert on that all important topic of the day. Or maybe it is watching the TV shows: the endless sports alternatives such as the "Dodge ball / Lumberjack biathlon"; documentaries including deep sea exploration with the latest discoveries of new fish species; or reruns of great cinematic achievements like Glengarry Glen Ross, The Godfather, Serpico, Scarface, or anything else with Al Pacino in it.

Beverage…check

A salt or sugar ridden snack…check

Positioning….feet up…head positioned directly at the TV…check

Remote…check

And then…You hear it!

Faintly at first….then the deft movement of your thumb activating the mute function, confirms it

Yes, you heard it!

The one word that creates more fear and anxiety than any other. Despite its simplicity it can unravel hours of planning. In its tone, it creates a level of anticipation to rival the last second three-pointer arcing toward the basket; the overtime field goal attempt in football; bases loaded, bottom of the ninth, full count pitch; or the Stanley Cup playoff overtime breakaway.

Its lack of specificity conjures a range of possibilities…all bad, comparable to being on the losing end or failure of the aforementioned athletic crescendos.

The Word:

"Honey?"

*Oh my God….**NO!***

Can't be…..Not allowed.

You knew you were in the clear.

You didn't have anything else to attend to.

But what has she come up with?

That woman that you married…seems to have a sixth sense…. that timing, the supernatural control…to be able to evoke such fear in that one word:

"Honey?" …that tone!

"Honey?"…that timing!

"Honey?"…How did she know you were just getting comfortable?

Now…what do you do?

— The nap strategy? (Twitching or not moving? Which will be most convincing? Control the breathing? Shallow or deep?)

— The "I am already involved with something incredibly important so don't come up with anything that is going to reprioritize my time" strategy?

What could it be? The dry cleaning needs to be picked up?…. that new couch needs to be seen?…a recital?…the out-of-town business associate that wants to go to dinner?…the historical tour of your hometown that she bought from the begging, sniveling little kid at the door two months ago…and the cocktail party afterwards?…. that BBQ at the neighbor's house that somebody insensitively scheduled for a Sunday afternoon…. YOUR Sunday afternoon?!

After everything you do, don't you deserve a break?

*Can't you be given the opportunity to **relax** and do your own thing without interruptions from others?*

*All you want is **your** down time.*

And not that you don't love your family and friends, but "My God, can't I get a little time for me?!"

* * * * * * * * * * * * *

Well, Buck, yes you can....but it is not an entitlement. **It is earned**. And not in the way you may think.

Look, you are married to a woman that you love. Yes, that feeling may have grown up as you did (hopefully), but she is the most important woman in your life. And in whatever way she may express it to you, and she is doing so every day of her life, you are the most important person in her life.

So how do you sync that deep feeling for her and the desire to fulfill **your** needs (no, not those)? With everything that is going on in your life, her life, and everyone else's lives that seem to be prioritized over yours, this may seem impossible. You just want balance and to be happy with life!

Well here's your starting point and the key to your happiness: **She is always right**. Yep, sorry..... no buts, no conditions, no qualifications...she is right and you need to get over it. The moment you do, your life has just made a huge turn for the better.

OK, I know there is a very large group of men out there that is preparing the noose for me, calling me some milquetoast metro (or worse), thinking that I am not a REAL man because I don't assert myself and "let her know who is Boss."

Best of luck gentlemen (term used loosely). Simply put, there are two kinds of men in this world: those that recognize the validity of my assertion and those that will EVENTUALLY recognize the validity of my assertion.

The purpose of this book is to help all of you, and in particular those of you showing resistance to this concept, by providing you guidance on how to earn your freedom and happiness… 'Win the War.' You do this by not only recognizing the righteousness of your wife in all things, but also doing a few kind things once in a while that will either elevate her to the stature she deserves, or make sure that she maintains the lofty position to which you have already raised her.

Am I intending to provide a How-to-Wuss-out guide? Absolutely not. While the old phrase "Happy Wife, Happy Life" applies, for those of you resisting it, some experienced guidance may help. I am providing a few suggestions on how to have **fun** in your marriage and maintain respect and consideration in the relationship. And yes, I'm also throwing out some good old fashioned, romantically-inspired mush to make your wife feel like a queen.

Guess what, Dorothy? We are definitely not in Kansas anymore. The world is a dangerous place. The stresses and strains on our familial and marital relationships are real and many. I am not a psychologist, psychiatrist, or marital / family therapist. I am just a regular guy whose inspiration for writing this book is the love of my wife and comments from her friends that I should provide lessons to their husbands on how to do a few nice things for them once in a while.

I am certainly no saint, but I can tell you that not a day goes by that I do not thank God that I am married to my wife and take a few minutes to reflect on what we have and what I can do to make it better.

Once in a while, I am successful.

As a result I am afforded the opportunity to engage in my manly pursuits and maintain a great relationship with my wife. And, by the way, my view of what is enjoyable and "manly" has expanded as a result. Yes, Hoss, Old Dogs can learn new tricks.

So read on and enjoy. If it doesn't work for you, fine. But just remember one thing: It **is** All About Her!

****

As you anticipate the words that may follow "Honey?" – the Honey-do list of home maintenance activities that you haven't touched for weeks; the unexpected chauffer duties about which you had no knowledge etc…she finishes the sentence,

"Honey? I am going out for a while, do you need me to get you anything at the store?"

As the Michigan fight song, "Hail to the Victors" begins to play in your head, you feel a little guilty for all of those negative alternatives you had been anticipating…

"No thanks. I'm good, Babe."

Welcome to the winning side.

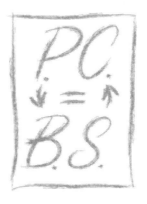

P.S... FOR OUR PURPOSES, PC IS BS

On my list of oxymorons, Political Correctness is at the top. This book may be viewed by some as insensitive to those whose preference is to marry someone of the same sex. I use the word *marry* to cover every word or phrase that is currently used to describe a relationship in which two adults have committed to each other.

Let me be clear, I am not making any statement on this subject at all. My personal opinion is that far too many people that have little or no knowledge of the perspectives and feelings of same sex couples are currently making far too many statements and judgments on the subject.

To quote a couple of our time's great poets, "Let it be." (Thank you John and Paul)…okay…so I made a statement…. couldn't help myself.

I am a heterosexual guy, writing about that which I have been told I have a fair amount of knowledge. I am endeavoring to share that knowledge in an entertaining way. In doing so, if I have failed on some level of political correctness, please forgive the absence of an apology. I simply ask for your appreciation of the fact that I am not attempting to speak about things I know nada about.

In an attempt to cover all my bases, as I suggest that women's partners treat them with a little more care and thoughtfulness, I realize there may be some women who interpret my assertions as demeaning to women. To them I say that there is a very good chance that the rest of this guide may not be for you: it gets worse. In my personal and professional life, there is no bigger advocate for the equality of women than I. If in your view of equality, my approach to fun, respect, and romance is inappropriate, nothing I can type here will change your view. And of course, you're correct (because you're always right).

With that said, I hope you will all still want to read on, as the concepts of respect, romance, and fun apply universally. As I mentioned earlier, the purpose of this book is to provide "a few suggestions on how to have fun in your marriage and maintain respect and consideration in the relationship." I would suggest that the concepts are consistent with any intimate relationship, even if some of the specific tactics may require modification.

WHO WE ARE

The unwritten history of failed marriages is strewn with the remains of men that were "dead right". This is the concept of having applied *perfect* logic to an *imperfect* situation in an *imperfect* world and as a result being left to wallow in the disappointment of their wives not accepting their *perfect* truth.

In fact there is no *right* answer. While logic has its place, it should only be applied when you have agreed on what the situation is and your objectives. In the absence of reaching this common ground, winning may be the acceptance that you are actually wrong. That's right, you are wrong. And a hearty congratulations to you, my Friend!

With all of the training from business, sports, schools, and social experiences that most of you have had, I am sure that in the midst of disagreement, you fall on the correct side your fair share of the time. But when it comes to the relationship with your wife, if you are not in agreement with your wife, you are probably wrong.

In actuality, if your marriage is built on any commonality at all, most disagreements involve relatively unimportant and non-actionable issues, in which the real difference in the positions of the two of you is relatively small.

> "I WISH THE PRACTICAL GUY, THE PASSIONATE GUY, THE EVEN-KEEL GUY, AND THE EXCITING GUY, COULD ALL HANG OUT TOGETHER." CATHY, MARRIED 3 YEARS*

Many of us feel this insatiable desire to "win," to be right for right's sake. But why? To exhibit that we **can** win? And what are we winning? Why? Who cares? The dog? If winning is that important to you, go cuddle up with your canine friend, as that is the warmest thing that you are going to experience in the foreseeable future.

Let's take a look at the situation a little differently, starting with YOU.

I have always thought that 1940s psychologist Abraham Maslow's Four Stages of Learning (Abraham Maslow) approach is an excellent structure for addressing a variety of business and personal situations. The Four Stages are:

1. **Unconscious Incompetence** The individual neither understands nor knows how to do something, nor recognizes the deficit, nor has a desire to address it.

2. **Conscious Incompetence** Though the individual does not understand or know how to do something, he or she does recognize the deficit, without yet addressing it.

---

* In order to get other voices in on this discussion, I scientifically (not) surveyed friends and co-workers, male and female, on what they love and would love to have more of in their relationship. While many of their thoughts are incorporated in this guide, some of their gems are highlighted throughout.

3. **Conscious Competence** The individual understands or knows how to do something. However, demonstrating the skill or knowledge requires a great deal of consciousness or concentration.

4. **Unconscious Competence** The individual has had so much practice with a skill that it becomes "second nature" and can be performed easily (often without concentrating too deeply). He or she may or may not be able to teach it to others, depending upon how and when it was learned.

With all due respect (and possibly apologies) to Dr. Maslow, I will briefly apply these concepts to the four types of married men in American Society. As soon as I type the phrase *American Society,* the perception may be that I have arrived at these categorizations through a life-long study of the human psyche with significant investigation into the male condition. Hell no! While I do pride myself on being an astute observer of people, **my** doctorate is in being a damn good husband, a title bestowed on me by my lovely wife.

Based on what category you fall into, you should take the information contained herein as anything ranging from specific instruction on how to take action quickly, to the suggestion of some new things to try, and everything in between.

Generally, married men fall into these four categories of marital and spousal awareness:

1. Unconscious Incompetent, aka **Clueless**: Yep you still exist...and in significant numbers. You don't get it and don't know that you don't get it. And that's why you don't get it....get it? You know you're in this category if your idea of an intimate gift is a set of tires; a romantic date is going out

together for drive-thru fast food; and the last time the words "I love you," passed through your lips was either in response to hearing it from your wife (with the obligatory "...too." added on) , or directed at your 60" Hi-Def Widescreen TV. There is very high likelihood that this guide was provided to you as a gift....with an unspoken, if not subtle, message. You aren't a bad person, you just may have your priorities focused in other directions.

1. Conscious Incompetent, aka **Wannabe**: You want to join in the game, but you don't know how to play. There is hope because you know that there is something you don't know! You are characterized by that awkward smile and flushed feeling you get when observing romantic or creative behavior being exhibited by other men. You may know who stars in _Chocolat_ and _The Devil Wears Prada;_ have a closet liking for chick flicks; but feign ignorance of the cinematic genre when in the presence of your Buddies. You may also have delved into the world of women's fashion in selecting gifts for your wife, but may still consider Nike, Adidas, and Reebok to be haute couture (look it up).

3. Conscious Competent, aka **Stud:** You have a standard set of deliverables for each occasion that get the standard positive response. You spend time thinking about your marriage, your relationship, and your wife. You ask yourself questions like: how do we improve upon what we have?; sometimes, how do we regain what we did have?; what can I do that would help my wife or really make her happy?; how can I show her I love her in a fun and/or romantic way? Oh, and you think through these, arrive at answers, and execute. You may have become predictable, but you are actually a pretty happy guy.

4. Unconscious Competent, aka **Romeo**: You are a natural. You get it and you know you get it. (And by the way, that's why you get it). It just comes to you either through natural romanticism or continual practice. In the moment, you always have the right words to say and you exhibit creativity in expressing your love to your wife. Your passion for your wife is clear and she appreciates your romantic nature.

Hopefully you have now identified where you are in these categories. But being the multi-talented, versatile guy that you are, you may be straddling a couple of them. Regardless of the category with which you identify, the forthcoming collection of thoughts is aimed at all four of you with a request that you consider taking the following actions:

Clueless: Wake up and get off your ass before it is too late.

Wannabe: Give it a shot and enjoy your new world.

Stud: Understand how to keep it going and expand your horizons.

Romeo: Well done, my Friend. You may find a few nuggets in here to use. Give yourself a pat on the back and help one of the other guys.

So read on McDough and have some fun with your new lifestyle.

WHO SHE IS

Who is this woman you married? She is complex, multi-faceted, and ever changing. No rocket science here, you knew this from the first time you believed that she either changed her mind or made an inexplicable (in your mind) decision. The challenge we have in fully grasping what makes our beauty tick is that we like things in nice logical boxes.... repeatable, predictable, and unsurprising. The problem with this is that first, we ain't gonna find this in the organism with the XX chromosome configuration, and second, even if we could, wouldn't that be boring and dull?

Instead, please let me suggest an alternate view of your world by introducing you to the many women to whom you said "I will," when you told your wife, "I do.".

THE LOVER

This is the woman that you viewed from afar, inspired you to summon the courage to ask her out, and joined with you in a passionate physical and psychological match. Where is that woman? She is probably sitting across the room from you now and sleeping beside you every night. If you haven't seen her in a while, don't despair, she is still there wanting to be desired.

OK, maybe the sex may not be as frequent (and this book is not going to cover that issue in any detail...I will leave that to Masters and Johnson, the Kama Sutra, and your imagination), but consider that it is not **her** testosterone level that has been steadily decreasing since age 18. It is not **her** love handles that made your guttage threshold (the age at which your waist and age are the same number) get pushed out 10 years. You have to admit, when it got easier to get, you may have become a little lazier about your presentation....and if this doesn't apply to you, well bully for you! Speaking of bull ...

The point is, The Lover is still there, she may just be hidden behind the school lunches, the occupation, the chauffer duties, and the various other jobs your wife has had to take up over the years. Seek and you shall find her.

The Partner

This is the woman that after your heart and loins calmed down, you envisioned as being the teammate with whom you could make a life. Depending on when you first saw your Partner, those dreams may have changed over the years. The key is that somewhere in your incredibly logical and dependent mind, you envisioned someone that would, and subsequently committed to, stay with you through thick and thin. And if you are like most people, you may have the feeling that it has been "thicker" than you thought it would be.

What is pretty cool is that you haven't been alone through those times, your Partner has been there with you.

Congratulations. She is still there, joining you in the things that neither of you probably expected that you would do in your life when you were in the dream state of your relationship. But as you continue the adventure of your life, you have both learned that the path has many turns...some fun and good...some not so fun and painful. But who has been there? Your Partner.

THE CAREGIVER

Any married man that has ever really left his mother, has looked for and found a "replacement" Caregiver. Let's not go down the path of the thought that you only have one mother and that no one can replace her...given.

But we are a dependent lot. If you don't suffer from the lowering-of-your-pain-threshold syndrome when your wife is present, you are always able to clearly articulate the incredible amount of pain that you are suppressing. If you are honest with yourself, the little boy inside of you still needs the feminine touch, word, thought, and action that is in the DNA of every woman.

And to whom do you turn when you are in need of this treatment? The person that has brought you ice-packs and heating pads when you were fully capable of getting off your fat derriere and securing it yourself; the darling chef that has re-written culinary history to create that which only you consider comfort food; and the Mother Teresa figure that has tolerated your periodic regression to the mentality of a 4 year old, as you so bravely fought off that bane of human existence, the common cold.

The Confidante

Remember that time that you shared the first secret, embarrassing event, or unpopular opinion with that woman that is accompanying you to your 1000th youth sporting event or artistic performance? She's the person who didn't judge you, didn't laugh, and whose trust you could always count on. Not sure who you run with, but there are not a lot of people on this earth that you can rely upon in that way. And in those situations in which YOUR female side makes a cameo appearance, and you just need to vent or express your feelings, I am guessing that your first choice isn't the guys walking up to the 1st tee with you on Saturday mornings or bringing the beer over for Monday Night Football. It's the woman who shares your name and life.

The Most Amazing Woman in the World

…and weren't you lucky for getting her! OK, clearly a certain amount of all of these people make up that rather complex woman you call your wife. The primary reason for her complexity is the burden she carries in caring for your fragile ego and managing your emotional state. Without these responsibilities, she would have only her own relationship challenges with which to deal. But she has taken on the incredible task of managing yours, as well. Not an easy chore, but one for which, whether you know it or not, you are very grateful.

Before you rush to arrange my flogging, consider these questions:

> To whom do you speak first when you have achieved a victory of any level of importance? Who acknowledges it and joins in your pride, regardless of the importance, and sometimes with little knowledge of the real importance?

> Who still expresses her appreciation of you as a physical specimen, regardless of the destruction that genetics and years of self-inflicted abuse and inactivity have wrought on your appearance? And why is the casual hint or supportive suggestion of how you could better take care of yourself usually tempered with such qualification as to hide what the objective observer might see?

> Who looks through all of the faults and sees the person that you really want to be, even when you may be light-years from that ideal? How many times have those conversations concerning your unrealized potential, that could have been incredibly ugly, been turned around by her to be a 'glass half-full' discussion, as opposed to the rather disheartening alternative?

I pose these questions, because I am convinced that there is either a class offered in elementary school that has been hidden from all males through a grand conspiracy; some form of divine or alien intervention; or a genetic wiring difference in women which enables then to know how to manage the male ego. And while this is executed with varying levels of sophistication and skill, it is a talent possessed by most women.

GIVE IT UP, BOYS

As I mentioned earlier, **she is always right** and it is this amalgamation of people which qualifies her to be so. Further, it makes sense for us to acknowledge her omniscience and interpersonal skills management capability by abdicating control of our lives to her. Once you do, your life becomes so much better.

Once you let go of the control handle, the innumerable question concerning social engagements, family choices, and personal preferences about which you have no informed opinion anyway, are no longer part of your responsibilities. This is not to say that all things should be removed from your visibility. The major issues for which you both share responsibility never go away, and you don't want them to. But it is pretty damn cool to have a personal manager and social director.

You still need to ensure that those activities you enjoy reserving for yourself are preserved, and that can be achieved through the trade-off for your tacit agreement on her leadership and organizational superiority with regard to the rest of your life.

> "MOST OF MY FRIENDS THAT HAVE A HAPPY MARRIAGE HAVE NO IDEA WHAT THEIR SOCIAL CALENDAR IS AND REALLY DON'T CARE. IT IS ONE LESS THING I HAVE TO WORRY ABOUT...AND WOULD IT BE ANY DIFFERENT IF I DID?" WILL, MARRIED 24 YEARS

If it is still not sinking in and you have ever golfed, equate this approach to the counter-intuitive concept that the easier you swing a golf club, the farther the ball goes. The less control you have over your life, the more of your life will be yours to control.

A reasonable man abdicates control. Check with any guy that has done this and he will tell you that his life has improved immensely, with a lingering question as to why he waited so long.

THE "WE" YOU TWO CAN BE

So Lads, there's the set-up.
She's always right….accept it
She's most qualified to have control….give it
And It's All About Her…..act on it!

The balance of this guide will share perspectives and actions for you to consider to let her know that It's All About Her, improve your relationship, and have some fun in the process.

FUNDAMENTAL THOUGHTS ON THE FUNDAMENTALS

Before we dive in, I want to share a few basic thoughts on some relationship fundamentals.

"Hello?"

The importance of being there…**being there for her** is numero uno. Having fun, entertaining, buying gifts, and creating special occasions mean nothing if you aren't there, physically and emotionally. Your taking the time to listen, being there emotionally, and, accepting her for all that she is, is the bedrock of the marriage…the rest is the icing on the cake.

"We are gathered here….".

I think most wedding ceremonies, including the ones I have presided over*, have some version of the taking

---

*Clarification time: I have conducted a few civil marriage ceremonies. While I do get a little "preachy" from time to time, I am not a minister.

one another "for better or worse" phrase in them. You and the rest of the Husband Fraternity tend to view that as the tactical, event-driven "better or worse". Well guess what? It also applies to emotional and personality-based "better or worse." It means that you are accepting of all the wonderful things that make up that woman you married and the not-so-wonderful things (nope, no list from me...you have your own). And the deal includes her friends, her relationships, and her family... everything. Oh and she's doing the same thing, by the way.

And as you go about your daily routines, remain open to the two-way communication that is at the center of any relationship. You know she is in your court so ask for her help as she asks for yours...but one note: DO NOT, repeat, DO NOT ask for her input or opinion and turn the conversation into a debate of whether she is right or wrong. IF you do, you will NEVER, repeat, NEVER get that honesty again. It is rare that you have the opportunity to get input from someone who is 100% behind your interests, your success, your self-fulfillment, and your happiness. So treat it with respect.

Your "taking each other" also means not only sharing things, but sharing of yourself emotionally...**your** emotional "better or worse." Now most of the time, you don't have to nudge your darling wife to go there...that place where emotions are freely acknowledged and experienced...she is usually way ahead of you. This includes both positive and negative moments. Clearly, we don't plan the sad events or the loss of loved ones, as you would a romantic evening, or a hobby or interest that you both enjoy. But when you hit a rough patch, be there, really there, and be you.

WHEN THE GOING GETS TOUGH, THE TOUGH STOP FIXING

Being the manly men we are, we have a tendency to want to address things in the Joe Friday approach: "Just the facts, Ma'am...just the facts." ... just solve things. There is no time in which our urge to be pragmatic and solve things needs to be suppressed more that in the situation of dealing with a personal loss to her or her emotional pain. Outside of logistics of certain situations associated with the loss of a friend or family member, emotions experienced and expressed are not solvable. They just are.

Your role as friend, coach, or observer during an emotional period is huge, as your Lovely may need to adjust to a new personal/emotional environment. In reaction to her circumstances, her behavior may change and you are probably one of the best people to fully observe the whole picture. But tread lightly and be gentle and caring.

OFF WE GO, INTO THE WILD BLUE YONDER...

With all that under our belt, here we go....a few suggestions around how to add fun, love, spice, acknowledgement, consideration and respect into your married life. Some of this is guidance, some is informational, and all is experiential.

And if you start feeling a tingling in your wallet, relax, Bubba. This is all about choices and alternatives, not mortgaging your future. The phrase, "you get what you pay for," does not apply to your wife. A good marriage cannot be bought. Many of the following suggestions create little or no financial burden, but they may require your **time and thought** — the two most valuable things you have to give.

And a message to you, whether you are Clueless, Wannabe, Stud, or Romeo: Enjoy it!

And by the way, Smile, dammit!

Right now!

Feel better? No?

Then picture your wife on your wedding day....now I gotcha.!

Lighten up, open your mind, and have some fun with this.

My sincere wish for you is that you share in some of the joy I experience every day.

Envy? C'mon, the joy is there for the taking...go for it!

All inclusive? Absolutely not. But after you have finished my attempt to share some of my favorites, if your competitive juices begin flowing and you feel compelled to poke holes in my approaches or find additional areas in which you could inject some excitement and fun, be cautious, my friend...you may have just bought into the game and be well on your way to Winning the War.

You are Married to the Most Wonderful Woman in the World....Now Let's See You Act Like it!

From Basic Good Form to Going for the Gold

ACTING LIKE IT (BECAUSE IT'S TRUE)

Let's just get to it Boys:

The Ring: Wear it.

The Door: It's there to be opened and you should do it — car, house, elevator…'nuff said. And while you are at it, extend the courtesy to others. She'll see it and appreciate it.

The Chair: It's there to be pulled out in preparation for her sitting in it. Follow this by helping her adjust it after she is seated. Very important here is to get the order correct. This is old school but still a show of class. Again, while a positive reflection on you, the primary interest here is that people see that SHE is respected, appreciated, and loved.

The Touch: Public displays of affection, subtle ones, are not only acceptable, but there is no better way to show the world that you hit the jackpot. You're quite willing to publicly deliver the handshake-to-right shoulder to right shoulder-half- hug thing and the endless varieties of fist punch and high 5's to your buddies, so I think we can agree that extending a little public touch to the babe you married is acceptable.

Holding hands may be considered by some to be childish or corny, but she isn't just somebody! She is your wife, and on this, it is very unlikely that she will turn you away. It's just a nice way of once again showing a little love and affirmation to your best friend.

Even just wrapping a couple of fingers with hers is still a way of showing that you are connected and that you are pleased with that situation. A hand on the elbow, a gentle arm around the waist…it all works. Essentially anything short of position 34 in the Kama Sutra sends the message to others, and most importantly to her, that she is special to you and life is damn good.

Formal occasions, regardless of the specific attire, are another time to show her the class that is inside of you. Take her hand and put it underneath and over your arm. Yes, if you aren't used to it, it may feel a little awkward, but get over it, if only to guarantee that extra time to see the replay of Top 10 plays on ESPN.

The Walk: Tradition has it that when walking/escorting your lady outdoors, you should always walk on the street side of her. This has evolved to walking on the side that protects her from the greatest potential of harm. Regardless, the suggestion is that you do walk with her at a reasonable pace, not behind her or ahead of her. An exception to this may be when you are performing the off-tackle run through the moving crowd and need to plow through the masses…. but still keep her close and hold her hand.

The Purse: Hold it.

** I should acknowledge here that there are some cultures in which it is expected that the woman always walk behind the man by a significant distance. I would bet that very few from those cultures would find value in what I suggest here, or in this book for that matter. For those of you to whom this applies, carry on, men…just one comment: check the date. My calendar says it's the 21st century….equality, suffrage, respect….read the definitions. Oh wait, that would require having your eyes open…apologies…maybe this is just my enlightened ignorance… but I digress. **

The Kiss: The delivery of a gentle kiss to the hand, cheek, forehead, or lips is another public declaration of the care you have for your wife and the value you have in your relationship. And by the way, it also works when you are in private. Just do us all a favor: we are all pretty sure that at this point in your relationship you are not virgins, but we really don't need to see your significant sexual prowess in a public display of foreplay. Nothing deserving an R movie rating, please.

✳ **The Affirmation:** Tell your wife that you love her once a day….and mean it.

The Argument: Lose it…and quick...Avoid the entire situation when you can and take responsibility to elevate the discussion to one that adults should have…not 12 year olds. (Oh, don't furrow your brow and frown like you have never fallen into that trap.) All of us have our disagreements and have experienced that awkward feeling when witnessing the public display of this behavior by others. As the football team calls its plays in the huddle, if you need to re-adjust your approach in public, drop back a few yards and discuss your next play privately, before coming up to the line again. We (and she) thank you.

The Date: Arrange it and treat her like it is your first date — until later(Yeah Baby). Make sure that once in a while you take control of the social event including where, when, and how. When applicable, also arrange for the babysitter.

Similar to the later discussion on shopping for her, expense need not be an issue here. It can be anything from scheduling a specific time to take a walk to the local coffee shop or park, to a formally arranged dinner at a romantic eatery. My mother In-law (great lady) has a phrase around dinner preparation that shows that someone was thoughtful — they "cared enough to warm the bread." Care enough to think through the detail and who knows, maybe something else will warm up later.

(see "Date" section in the Chapter **The Pampered Chief**)

The Look: 90% of communication is non-verbal, and often times what is communicated without words is far more powerful than verbal communication. A smile, a wink, an eyebrow raised in acknowledgement of that woman next to you, or across the room, says more than you can imagine.... oh yes, and make sure the target of these gestures is YOUR WIFE.

The Flirt: Get caught checking your wife out. This should not require much effort, just take a little 10-second trip down fantasy lane. Common responses to this behavior are your wife giving you that return smile; the sly eyebrow raise; the old head raise-acknowledgement; and sometimes the ultimate non-verbal (not always) activity...but I am not going there. That's for you two.

Again the whole idea is to have some fun with it and make sure that she continues to see that you still believe in your heart that you really care and desire her...because you do!

Remember when I described all those women you married? If you are challenged on the flirtation/fantasy front, give these a shot:

Fantasize about Your Lover

Acknowledge Your Partner

Appreciate Your Caregiver

Share with Your Confidante

&

Hit on The Most Amazing Woman in the World!

A FLOWER A DAY KEEPS THE LAWYERS AWAY

Women like receiving flowers. Now there is a revelation right up there with the Cubs are not going to win the World Series; hockey and basketball players will respond to being penalized with a shake of their head and that incredulous look; soccer players will be sprawled on the pitch from the force of an opponent's breath; everyone has inhaled; and the sun is going to rise in the East and set in the West. That being said, allow me to ease you into my world by sharing some thoughts about the floral gift.

Buy flowers for no occasion. You don't need one. You are married to the perfect woman: show her. Direct enough?

And there is a reason to do this: She is who she is. This is pretty simple stuff. Today is Thursday, in the middle of April..... nice day outside....I needed to head out to the optometrist to get my eyes checked and run a couple of errands. As I was heading back, I thought of my wife. Nice thoughts. There is a florist about ½ a mile away from the house...Alexandria's. One of my wife's favorite flowers is pink roses. Stopped by, got a dozen, and brought them home. Why? Because the smile on her face when she sees them is worth it to me. No occasion. Just because......

It doesn't have to be roses and they don't have to be from a florist. Showing up at the door with a $3.99 bouquet from the local grocery store can have the same effect. For the price of a gallon of gas, you can brighten your wife's day. It is just a simple and effective way of saying "I thought about you today." The more random and the more unexpected, the greater the impact.

Buy flowers for an occasion. Flowers are a great way to communicate your feelings to your wife. They are expected on the obvious — anniversaries and birthdays. Failure to execute on these days is the relationship version of Newton's 3rd law of motion: To every action there is always an equal and opposite reaction (now I can say that this guide has been elevated to a scientific level). Don't miss these opportunities!

Hint[1]: Write the occasion down on your calendar 3 days before the date. Hint[2]: If you are traveling or too busy to get out, 1800flowers .com, Teleflora.com, or FTD.com are very convenient, they have great suggestions on the specific arrangement, and a wide-range of prices.

In addition to these occasions, think about holidays, particularly those that traditionally attract all of those wonderful relatives of yours that love to descend on your house. When selecting flowers for these times, consider something that may also double as a centerpiece for that occasion…c'mon, you're the one that prides himself on being logical and knows the value of having multiple uses for things (think duct tape). Buy them for her, but select for the occasion.

If I haven't convinced you yet, you miser, look at it this way: She is probably going to buy something anyway, why not get the jump on it and make her day?

I will speak to your involvement in general party planning later and your proficiency in the floral area may prove to be helpful there as well.

"THE PHONE RANG AND IT WAS MY MOM. SHE THANKED ME FOR THE FLOWERS, TO WHICH I REPLIED, 'WHAT FLOWERS?' MY HUSBAND HAD SENT THEM; I THINK I'LL KEEP HIM!" JULIE, MARRIED 5 YEARS

Make up a reason to buy flowers. Every victory or triumph has historically been commemorated through the giving of floral or plant arrangements…reference laurel leaves from the Greek and Roman tradition…and just a quick elaboration here: "resting on your laurels" was coined to suggest that one not bask in the glory of past accomplishment, as laurel leaves were traditionally worn by Emperors, heroes, poets, etc. No, "laurels" are not a reference to the two lobes of your buttocks.

Celebrate the occasions of your relationship.

Celebrate your happiness.

Celebrate Her: Celebrate her accomplishments, not the least of which may be dealing with you 24/7 365 days a year. Again, this does not need to be overdone or become a financial burden. It can be anything ranging from the sun coming up in the morning, to surviving a summer with kids home from school every day, to an accomplishment at her work. Pick your spots, and have some fun with it. Just be prepared: smiles, hugs, kisses, and once in a while, tears may be forthcoming.

Advanced degree: Buy cut flowers and arrange them yourself. Okay maybe this is a stretch and if I am losing you manly men here skip the next few sentences. A few tries at it and/or a few minutes' reviewing the basics from books or the websites referenced at the end of this guide, on the art of flower arranging might actually result in you discovering a hidden talent. It's not like you have to be a Michelangelo. Hell, the flowers bring the color, texture, and form to the party....you just have mix and match, and deal with height and density. (Apologies to my professional florist friends.... it is indeed an art and requires training and experience to be good, but there are a few guys out there worthy of recruiting and I don't want to squelch their interest.)

OK...those of you that I lost...come back now.

THE PAMPERED CHIEF (AND IT'S NOT YOU)

Pamper, v. **to treat lavishly**: to lavish attention on somebody, indulging his or her taste for luxury; **gratify**: to indulge or gratify a desire or need. One of the most romantic and nicest things you can do for your best friend is to treat her to something…anything. What does she view as luxury? If she could do anything for an afternoon, what would it be? What enables her to relax and refresh?

The options here are endless, but as with everything we have been discussing, it's all about her perception. It may be the simple act of taking the kids to the park for an afternoon, so that she can just chill. It may be a few hours at a spa, a country walk…anything! Your role is to identify her idea of pampering and pave the way for her experiencing it.

Some Lavish Suggestions

The Rub: Similar to the buying of flowers or any gift, pampering need not be expensive. The only thing that is rarer than a woman declining the offer to have her shoulders or feet massaged, is the offer of that massage by her husband. While formal training is not required, reading up on it a little doesn't hurt. And if you listen to the "client", you will naturally get better at it.

> "He knows I've been pretty stressed these last few days at work and I woke up to him doing reflexology on my feet....it was pretty awesome." Laura, married 3 years

If to this point the extent of your physical contact has been sexual, understand that massage need not be sexual; if it turns into that, so be it, but the purpose here is just to provide the physical and emotional relaxation that comes as a result of the activity. There is also a value to having physical contact that is not directly tied to sex, but again in this area I defer to the professionals.

The Ladies Day/Night Out: One of things that your wife, and you to a certain extent, can lose when you get married and particularly when you have kids, is the relationship with your friends. Not necessarily that you aren't social with other couples and families, but with all the activities and obligations in our lives, the male/female need for gender-based camaraderie may not get satisfied. From a woman's perspective, one of the great ways that you can provide her with the opportunity to fulfill that need is by being supportive of the Ladies Night or Day out. Your support of this activity not only helps her, it sends a message that you are sensitive to how she ticks and what makes her happy.

> "THE BI-WEEKLY GATHERING OF THE JUGS (JUST US GIRLS) SEEMED LIKE A PAIN AS I DEALT WITH A FEELING OF ABANDONMENT. THEN SHE HOSTED ONE OF THE NIGHTS AND I OBSERVED THE TOTAL ENJOYMENT 8 WOMEN GAINED FROM JUST HANGING OUT TALKING ABOUT EVERYTHING UNDER THE SUN.... HMMMM....AN AWFUL LOT LIKE MY TEE TIME ON SUNDAY."
> DAVID, MARRIED 32 YEARS

The Spa

The Massage: Whether it is purchased by you or delivered by you, it is a sure winner. Sometimes a gift certificate at a local day spa is appropriate. Don't worry about getting specific with the gift certificate; she will be able to determine what she wants. You might also try having a masseuse make a visit to the house, giving her the comfort of home and no need to drive herself home afterwards.

The Pedicure/Manicure, or the absolute ultimate: The Mani-Pedi (ask her to explain): If your wife usually does her own nail grooming, a salon visit may be a treat. If she goes to a salon regularly, think spa and perhaps combine with another service.

Spa vs. salon is a bit like getting the invite to the exclusive golf club. It's still a round of golf, but the environment may be quite different from the local muni.

If you go the spa route, you can up the ante by involving one or more of her friends. This group activity is not just an extension of female pack behavior, like when they go to the ladies room en masse at a restaurant. It is more similar to how guys rarely get 1 ticket to a game or head over to a car show by themselves. There is some intrinsic value to being able to share the experience, regardless of how many times you have done it, with another person.

While you may have purchased a gift card for the spa for her, you shouldn't be expected to cover the cost of the services for the other members of the party. If finances allow, a nice touch would be picking up the tab for lunch/dinner for the party. As I have mentioned before, presents/luxuries should not create a financial burden. Find your wallet's comfort zone and stay there.

In addition to the previously mentioned services, there are all kinds of scrubs, steams, and polishes for face and body. Some are truly functional and physically therapeutic, others may be cosmetic. The key here is that she can periodically get what truly relaxes her and makes her feel special.

The Dinner: Depending on what arrangement the two of you have, fixing dinner for her, and the rest of the clan, may also be an appropriate luxury. If the kids are not a factor, doing this can also get into the Date arena. Regardless, the key here is that if it is unusual for you to do this, then **do it**, and do it thoroughly. By this I mean the shopping, the preparation, the serving AND the clean-up. It kind of takes away the value if you serve this nice dinner and she ends up having to clean-up. For you football fans, it's like entering the red zone and not scoring any points.

The kind of dinner is not important; the fact that you took responsibility for the whole enchilada (ouch) is what is important. It can be as simple as a variety of appetizers or a nicely-prepared salad, or as grand as a four-course gourmet meal. Whatever you are comfortable with will hit the mark, as long as she doesn't have to lift a finger, just a fork.

The Date

Simple: It really doesn't matter where, when, how or why. All that is important is the "you and her" part. It can be a movie, a walk in the park, a dinner at a nearby hamburger joint. What is important is that it is a DATE — you ask her, she accepts, and you go. Go out there and act like you are not married, just lovers, boyfriend/girlfriend.

It is amazing what the experience can yield — a new plan to address a problem or a dream; an opportunity to discuss something that has been avoided for a while; communication, by either of you, of feelings that had not been expressed before; a sharing of perceptions of current events that either impact you or have touched you deeply; recollection of fond memories; or rekindling feelings that you have for one another that haven't been expressed for a while due to all the stresses, strains, and distractions of everyday life. You don't have to plan for any of this. Just let it flow like you did years ago when you were dating.

Expense is no object — meaning that if you are on a tight budget, choose an activity that fits into that budget so that when you are on the date, the pinch is not on your mind. The only thing that should be on your mind is the two of you. Also try to set it up so that you are not constrained by time, allowing the date to go wherever it takes you.

> "HE SHOWED UP AT THE DOOR, WITH A SINGLE ROSE; HE GAVE
> ME 10 MINUTES TO GET READY; AND WE WENT OUT TO DINNER. I
> CAN'T EVEN REMEMBER WHERE WE WENT...IT DIDN'T MATTER."
> PAULA, MARRIED 12 YEARS

One thing I'd suggest, particularly if it has been a while since you two were out as a couple alone, is that you have a plan or an idea on where you are going to go. "Where do you want to go?" was probably not the way you approached your first date together. Give it a shot and if she comes back with a different idea or preference, be flexible enough to accommodate that idea, because as I hope you know by now, she **is** always right.

Extravagant: budget allowing, pull out all of the stops once in a while. Whether it is a surprise or fully disclosed, plan an elegant evening for the two of you. Just as fabulous is in the eye of the beholder when it comes to appearance, elegant is whatever it is to **her** — a restaurant, the symphony, a play, a concert, an evening in "the City" (how San Francisco is referred to in Northern California).

A couple of the best extravagant dates I have ever been on were rock concerts (The Killers & Green Day...highly recommended for those of you wondering if rock music died after 1980). Extraordinary seats, stretch limo, the whole nine yards as in party like a rock star. Truth be told, my wife actually arranged those and took me. Yes, it can work both ways, but why not make the first move?

If your destination or activity is to be a surprise, make her comfortable by letting her know a couple of details concerning attire and timing. If you have really gone nuts and purchased her attire for the evening, remember to allow a few days for her to make sure that she is completely comfortable with your selection, or replace it (which, as I will explain in the next section, does not diminish the value of your gift.)

If possible, arrange for transportation (taxi/limo/town car) for the evening or day. Should the two of you want to imbibe, you need not worry about your blood chemistry and you can just concentrate on the chemistry between the two of you. But more importantly, you can concentrate 100% on her and not be concerned with directions or driving.

Again, splurging is relative and you can pull this off and still keep your finances in shape. Clearly this is not a weekly, maybe not a monthly, occurrence. The key is to do something as special as she is once in a while.

Good friends and neighbors of mine, the Villotts, have a saying in their family that "life is about making memories." Take her out and make a memory!

The Weekend: the Weekend Getaway is another pampering option that can be as involved or simple as you want to make it. Depending on where you choose to go, you can combine the date and spa aspects into one. On the other hand, you can also make it as simple as going out to dinner at some remote locale and spending the night.

*****Advanced degree**…arrange a whole Vacation. A business associate shared with me that once a year her husband tells her when and the general climate and activity detail of their destination and he handles the rest. (I'm not worthy, Romeo!) Very cool and if you could have seen the way she lit up when she shared this with me, you'd know how worth the time and effort it was for her husband. I can't even recall if she told me where he had taken her. I don't think it mattered. She was just so proud and excited by the concept.

I am not suggesting that this must be an annual event, by any means, but the concept is there for the taking. It really doesn't even have to be a surprise to be effective. As with all things involving your wife, it is clearly the thought and effort which sends the message and creates the opportunity for the two of you to connect and enjoy each other.

✳ **Nice Touch Alert**: remember that whole thing about flowers? Of course you do! If you are staying at a hotel for any length of time, a couple of days prior to your arrival arrange to have a nice seasonal bouquet of flowers to be waiting in the room when you arrive.

The Lifetime: simple things that you can do periodically that make her feel special. I know we are all insanely busy, but how much effort is involved in you making and serving her coffee in the morning? Is there **something, anything,** that you can identify in your daily, weekly, or monthly routines that might be an opportunity for role reversal?....Is there a duty (nothing that is going to threaten your manhood) that would take the load off of her once in a while? You will be surprised how greatly appreciated a 20 minute give-back of previously planned time will be.

"BREAKFAST IN BED...LUNCH IN BED....DINNER IN BED. I JUST LOVE HIS CHOICE OF VENUES." WENDY, PARTNERING FOR 22 YEARS

The Card: Very similar to flowers, but less expensive and more varied. Funny, serious, or passionate, it is amazing the impact that a simple greeting card can have. And again, as with flowers, the more disconnected the timing is from a specific event or occasion — Valentine's Day, Anniversaries,

Birthdays, etc, — the better. The message, regardless of what the card says, is "I am thinking about you."

Putting your own touch on a card is also important. Rarely does a card send the complete message. It is entirely appropriate to have some fun either augmenting the message on a card with your own hand-written message, or even editing the card to fit your purpose. Personalizing shows you actually read the damn thing and thought specifically about her.

The Barry White Option: You don't have to be Shakespeare to create your own message. You have the passion and you speak and write the language. All that remains to qualify you is your expertise in the subject matter — **her**. You are, therefore, qualified to write poetry or prose and create your own message.

It may not be time to quit you day job and try to make a living from your skill with iambic pentameter (look it up. I did). But perfection is not the object of the exercise. The objective is to bring to light what your feelings are for your wife, period. She really doesn't care how good it is. She cares that you took the time to put into words how you feel about her. There are very few things more intimate than this. Suggestion: Start with "I Love You," and wrap around it one reason why and you are on your way, you romantic devil.

The KISS (Keep it Simple Stupid): The yellow sticky on the cabinet (or anywhere) that says "I love you".

Your Turn: It's now up to you!

53

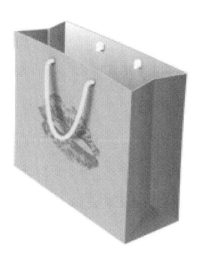

YOU CAN'T BUY LOVE...

BUT YOU STILL NEED TO SHOP

Of the various things that I do for my lovely wife, shopping for clothes is probably the one that gets the most positive reaction from her and her friends. This is not just blatant materialism and I am not a shill for the retail industry. Attire is an expression of the image that a person is trying to project. It is a very personal thing. Given that this is particularly true with your wife, to attempt to please her by selecting items for her wardrobe can be very rewarding, but is accompanied by a degree of risk. So, I submit to you some guidance concerning the sartorial gift.

It doesn't need to be expensive, but it must be fabulous! Clothing and accessories (...not choices of new car features or gaming options, but add-ons to basic outfits that accentuate the clothing and bring attention to specific aspects of the person wearing the outfit) need not be expensive. This is not to say that these gifts can't get pricey. Trust me, you can easily move from 2-digit to 4-digit or 5-digit prices, but it is not necessary.

While clothing need not be expensive, it should be distinctive. I do not mean that you have to buy your lovely a one-of-a-kind dress. While to do so will definitely send the appropriate message that you believe she truly is one-of-a-kind, there are very few of us that have the means to do this. You can send the same message by selecting something that is of your choosing and will be great for HER. When she puts it on, it **is** one-of-a-kind.

Distinctiveness and Fabulousness are in the eyes of the beholder. She is distinctive and fabulous. Add to it by selecting something that helps the rest of us less familiar with her, to see it.

It really is The Thought that Counts. Buy with a purpose, i.e. buy for an occasion or a place that the two of you like to go regularly...there is nothing better than hearing those words, "I could wear this to dinner with the Avrietts and Marshalls." Or "this would be perfect for work." By the way; if she thinks it is more appropriate for some occasion that is different than you had in mind when you bought it, know what? You got it...she's right!

If you see something that you think she is going to look killer in and you just don't have the occasion planned for her to wear it....create the occasion. It is strongly suggested that you allow for return time prior to the event, if a specific date is involved, e.g. vacation/show tickets, etc.

"Your mission, Mr. Phelps, is to infiltrate the perilous worlds of women's fashion and the retail industry, return with an extraordinary selection; and live to tell about it. As always, should you be caught or killed, the Secretary will disavow any knowledge of your actions."

I suggest you start by gathering some strategic and tactical intelligence prior to your mission. On the strategic side, think about the image that your wife has or is trying to establish. In various social and business situations, what do her clothes project? Classy, playful, sophisticated, sexy, conservative, or avant garde may all play into certain situations. Pick the area that most immediately comes to mind and try to match that in what you select.

On the tactical side, you must conduct a covert mission by surreptitiously entering the inner-sanctum of Her Majesty's closet. Check out what she has and based on what you think you are going to shop for, check out styles, sizes and fabrics. Also, particularly check out the brands of her nicer clothing. This will help you in selecting not only the right size, but also brands that are consistent in terms of style and quality.

This last step is not intended to prepare you to duplicate that which you have already discovered. It is intended to provide you with the basic knowledge on top of which you will add your creativity. Your wardrobe may be characterized by duplication and consistency. Break away from the confines of your manly paradigm and direct your efforts to provide some excitement, diversity, and fabulosity for Her.

Creativity Alert: As you start to visualize where you are going to go on this mission, a slight word of caution: there is a difference between Stylish and Slutty and it is important to go with the former and steer clear of the latter. If you are challenged in understanding the difference, here a few thoughts to ponder:

You'll know that your selection is in the *Sluttish* category if the result of your wife wearing the outfit is:

- Nothing is left to the imagination

- Her stride is reduced to 4"

- Somebody asks her how much, and they are not referring to the outfit

- Her girlfriends quit calling her, but **your** friends start

- She is brought in for questioning just for walking down the street

- Her hemline is confused with her waistline

- She can't wear in front of the kids and must wait for them to go to bed before she can put it on

At the other end of the spectrum, you'll know that your selection is in the *Stylish* category if the result of your wife wearing the outfit is:

- Her girlfriends asked where she got it

- She's told she has good taste

- People start humming "Pretty Woman" when she passes by

- She is looked at, not gawked at

- She is referred to as:

- o Vivacious (not Vavavoooom)

- o Edgy(not over the edge)

- o Polished (not blinding)

- Her friends ask her to help them with their style

- Her friends ask if you can help their husbands

- Her friends suggest that you write a book…..

FINAL NOTE FROM THE PREP FILE

I learned early in my business career that if you want to know how to run your business, ask your customer. It is entirely appropriate, to ask your wife what she likes. Whether she is watching a show or reading a fashion rag, ask her opinion on what she is seeing. Oh and by the way, if your inquiry about her style/taste comes on the heels of a compliment on how good she looks in what she is wearing, you will not only be more likely to get an honest response, but will have also sent a pleasing affirmation, you Sly Dog.

Off You Go!

Shopping is not like driving…ask for directions. Selecting clothing as a present requires thought and like many manly pursuits, requires practice. I strongly suggest you ask for help. You will find that most women (or men) working in a women's clothing store are very willing to help you through the process. If the person you are speaking to is not willing to work with you, ask to get help from someone else…people who are good at it are generally very willing to help and conversely, reluctance to help you is a sure sign that they are not that talented. For the mark-up you are paying on clothing, you deserve and should expect help.

Your salesperson should be able to provide you alternatives relative to shape/cut, size, fabric/weight, color, pattern, outfit combinations, and accessories (and more information on this can be found in the reference materials at the end of the guide). Often you will also find the staff willing to model pieces that you are considering. By this I mean the basics of holding the clothing up to themselves so you can evaluate the garment against skin shade, hair color, and size. Rarely will you find your wife's twin at the local women's boutiques, but you will find this approach to picturing your wife in the outfit very helpful.

There is another helpful resource in stores that you may have not considered, yet are influenced by every time you walk in the door: mannequins. While in various shapes and sizes, these 'models" give you an idea of outfit possibilities and potential combinations. While a little short on advice, their silent suggestions may provide you with excellent guidance.

A little caution here: No woman is thrilled by the comment from one her friends that "You know, I just saw that outfit on a display at J.C. Penney." Nothing against J.C. Penney, mind you, but pieces from a store display or our silent models are one thing, getting the whole enchilada this way is another matter. It's better to punt than mail-in the effort here.

A note on Age Appropriateness

Another caution as you start out is to be aware that, as stated before, you are contributing to your wife's expression of her image in what you select. You may also be helping her establish what that image or "style" is. In addition to your thoughtfulness, your activity here is also sending a message about how YOU see her.

For those of you in the 25 and older set, she isn't 18 and, unless you are inspired by the exclamation of "Gawd" and the repeated use of the bridging phrase, "You know," you don't want her to be.

IF she is 18, well good luck with that. For the rest of us, a woman can look current, stylish, attractive, playful, sexy, and any other way, without attempting to wear that which is just too young for her. Chances are it probably won't fit appropriately, and wearing clothes that are not age-appropriate can send a message that she is not only not comfortable with her state in life, but is desperately attempting to regain her younger years. Let's help her capture the joy in the here and now. Remember that's where you are — and she is with you.

Ladies, take what you will from these statements. If you disagree, well, okay, you're right....nope...sorry...not on this one, and you may not be running with friends that are being honest with you.

On the other side of this equation, is the concept of Drab (def. (noun): uninteresting to look at because of a lack of color or brightness; lacking interest, enthusiasm, or excitement). This is not acceptable....ever! Don't contribute to it. Unless you are aroused by Andy Taylor's Aunt Bea back in Mayberry, just don't go there!

THE NUMBERS GAME

Don't panic on the size issues...over time you will get the hang of it and if you get it wrong, it is OK. Your G-2, referenced earlier, will be helpful here. And if you do get it wrong, the following section will help you through the situation.

> ** A comment on purchasing clothing online: Until you have experience for size and fit, I would suggest that you use the online experience to identify trends and gather ideas. The risk of missing the mark and having to deal with the return hassle may not be worth the convenience. However, once you are in tuned with brands, size and style, have at it. The inventory and ease associated with online shopping is incredible and is perfect for those of you that experience an allergic reaction to shopping in public.*

RETURNING TO THE SCENE OF THE CRIME

Fear of failure has squelched many a man's realization of his dreams. Let's not let that creep into this, as here it is impossible to fail. Even if your 'Hit Rate' (size, style, color, fabric...hell, she likes/loves it) is only 50%, that is still pretty good.

If the miss has to do with size, it is the same as a pitcher missing a strike high or low....doesn't really make any difference, it is still just a ball (as long as it is not a wild pitch). But in this game, you are always ahead in the count and the game.

You do, however, want to be prepared for a couple of common reactions to size misses:

> The **"Oh, so you think I'm that big?!"** reaction: a possible emotional response to a size miss that is larger than she is. Your initial inclination in response to this may be to explain away the mistake...STOP! Do not Pass Go! Do Not

Collect $200! You need not say anything, just fast path to the next session and recovery is assured...well pretty much assured. If you just HAVE to respond, let her know that in the store it looked smaller and you were under the impression from the salesperson that the brand ran small. You can always also appeal to her practical side and suggest the tailoring option, if the garment is tailorable. This most likely applies to pants (you gutsy SOB), and it is always easier to take something in than to let it out. Here, as with many things in life, less is more...don't try to "solve" anything, just move forward to your opportunity.

The **"Oh, so you thought I would fit into this?!"** reaction: usually an emotional response to a size miss that is smaller than she is. Your initial inclination in response to this may be to explain away the mistake...STOP! Do not Pass Go!.... Go directly to the next paragraph. Responding to this question is like answering the question, "Do these pants make my butt look fat?" There is no right answer and any response is likely to take you down (and I mean down) a path of conversation that has no upside.

Any miss, be it due to size, style, color, fabric, or atmospheric interference from solar flares is not a failure. The reality of the situation is that the worst that can happen is that she will need to return the present to the store. Okay, so? Now this is an important point: the key here is that if what you selected misses the mark, she will need to go to the store and find something different. **She will have to spend time on herself.** My guess is that your wife busts her tail for you. What you may view as a failure is really leading to your being successful in forcing **her** to spend time on **her**.

This last point is particularly important if you have children. When your wife, working outside of the home or not, makes life all about the kids and you, you need to help **her** make time for **her**. This is not a suggestion, it is an imperative, whether you are a fashionista or not.

Opportunity alert! Go the extra mile. Take the time to go shopping with her when she returns the item(s). Doing so shows that you care, and you will learn something about her tastes and fitting issues. Most importantly, you will be spending time with her doing something she enjoys and showing that it is all about **her**.

Make it a date…buy lunch…take your time, as with a number of very important things, slower is better.

It is better to have bought and lost than to have never bought at all.

Oh don't get me wrong, hanging around a fitting room or watching the search through the clothing racks can be tedious and boring. But so what? So are parts of the *Godfather* trilogy, *Independence Day, Gladiator,* and *Casino,* but that hasn't kept you from watching them 20 times (or more).

Most importantly, it is about **her** and she is worth it.

For those of you that have interest in diving deeper into this area, check out the *style* reference materials at the end of the guide.

BE THE HOST THE HOSTESS WITH THE MOSTESS DESERVES

Her Plan will always work…your job is to make sure it does: the more you team with one another, the better the results. In preparation for this section I collaborated with the best party planner and most gracious hostess I have ever met: my wife.

For starters, aim for balance in each other's responsibilities so that you throw the party *together*. Identify and separate the things that you each like to do, and the things you will do well as those usually go hand in hand. Then what is left needs to be divided to balance the available time and effort of each of you. It may get a little stressful, but just remember two things: 1. Breathe…all things work better with oxygen, and 2. Act like adults. It is only a party and it is meant to be **fun**. Try your damndest to make the throwing of it fun as well (testing the loud music and beverage menu prior to the party may be helpful here).

There are 7 basic stages for any party: Planning & Preparation, The Arrival/Welcome, Socializing[1], Serving, Socializing[2], Wind-down/Goodbye, and Clean-up. As your Complication Meter starts ringing, consider that even the casual get together

65

has these steps in it, and the cycle holds true and is repeated time over time, thousands of times per day across America, from sports-watching parties to the che'che' country club set.

To be sure, you have the capacity to up our game from your roaring twenties and can deliver outstanding results based on whatever kind of occasion you plan. With that wonderful teammate that you married, and with a little collaboration, any get-together can be a success. The style of the party can be from completely casual to formal. The approach is still the same, just the content may change.

Sitting down with your wife and thinking through what you want to do is essential. It can be as brief or as involved as the style of party you are hosting dictates.

On Help: The hiring of a Party Planner, bartender(s), and /or wait professionals is helpful, if affordable, but we're not going to go there for this guide. However, the local late teens/early 20's, related to you or not, can be very helpful and your engagement of them at a reasonable rate of pay, will certainly make you very popular in the neighborhood. You just need to be very specific on time and responsibilities with these willing amateurs.

The Anal Retentive Party Planner's Highlight Reel of Party-throwing: At a high-level, here are some considerations on how to ensure that two of you pull it off and remain a happy couple:

PLANNING PREPARATION

- The Checklist...create one, it helps.

- The Budget...create a ballpark estimate and add 20-30%. If expense is a consideration adjust DOWN to the level of comfort. You will not impress anyone and your darling wife will not enjoy herself, if the dollars involved are too high. If your original ideas are too expensive, recalibrate and / or share the burden with another couple.

- Guest Participation—know the answer to the question, "What can I bring?" You know the question is coming and if you are open to people participating, keep track of it. The last thing you need is 5 desserts and no salad.... well maybe a bad example, but I think you get the idea.

- Menu

  o Food—if dinner is part of the party, know if there are dietary issues for the guests and plan accordingly. Keep it simple and something that is not an experiment, unless you two are really accomplished chefs, the guests are really good friends, or you are **really** good with contingency plans.

  o Beverage- it is YOUR party and your call as to what is to be served. You are under no obligation to offer a full service bar, unless you want to. If this area is creating complication, go with fewer choices and better quality. Regardless of what you are serving, it's important that you always provide non-alcoholic alternatives.

o Serving and Consumption Tools: Platters, dishes, bowls, glasses, utensils, etc. Think through it... crunch the numbers, and add 20%.

• Shopping List: Often the person responsible for a given part of the party is responsible for the shopping for that part...depending on your ability to create accurate shopping lists, consolidating your shopping requirements can be a big time saver.

• Entertainment: your call as to how far you take this, but whether you are playing music from your own audio system or hire entertainment, think how it is adding to the party and not distracting from the socializing you want to take place, and your involvement in it. Also make sure that your, and most importantly your wife's, involvement with taking care of this is minimal during the party...from your guests' perception, it should just appear to happen.

• Guest List

o Mixology (n. the science of determining the most compatible make-up of attendees to a social gathering): We all have friends that span many interests and personalities. If diversity is important and encouraged, social toxicity can be tragic and must be avoided. Your party is not the time to play peace-maker for people that do not care for one another. While drama at a social occasion may frequently occur, let it be a surprise and not part of the plan. Attempting to engineer drama by selecting guests that have a high likelihood to have conflict, is flirting with disaster.

o   Invitations: whether verbal, written, or electronic, just make sure you have a way for your guests to let you know if they are coming and that a few days prior to the party, you know who and how many are planning to attend.

- The Environment

  o   Seating: decide how much you need, and if a combination of standing and sitting is ok.

  o   Ambiance. lighting, flow, music, entertainment, decorations, if applicable, etc.

  o   Conversation Areas…just know where you expect these to be. This is particularly important if you are entertaining in tight quarters and want to ensure that people have access to other essentials, like food, drink….bathrooms.

  o   People and Serving Flow….similar to above, think through how you want it to flow and it if it is not incredibly intuitive (most times not), you can let people know the approach in the later steps.

- Complete as much as possible the day before

  o   Food…prepare as much as you can the day before to reduce stress/activity levels the day/evening of the party. Desserts, appetizers, and dish ingredients are examples of common things that can be done ahead of time.

    o   Cleaning…be reasonable and share the fun here.

- Check in with the Boss…"Are you ready?" If she isn't what can you do to help her get that way?

The Arrival/Welcome

- First Impressions…you only get one shot here so make sure that the first impression for a guest arriving at your home is a positive one. Not sure if you are familiar with the positive impressions that flowers can make but……

- Mi Casa, Su Casa…let them know that it is their home for the next few hours and that you are very pleased that they are there.

- Last but not least, let your guests know who the brains of the outfit is and if you are the one greeting them at the door, that SHE will either be there shortly, or where she can be found.

Socializing[1]

- Facilitate guest introductions. For a party based out of your home, everyone should get the opportunity to meet the other guests.

- Beverages…let everyone know what is being served and how they can get it…best case is that you get it for them, but at a minimum, make sure they get pointed in the right direction.

- Guest Contentment…check in to make sure that people are enjoying themselves, including your wife.

o Being the real "Life of the party" is hard work, but well worth it….and the life of the party truly is not the center of attention…it is the center of the **facilitation**. Not that you need to be a wallflower, but hosting a party is taking on the responsibility of ensuring that every one of your guests enjoys his/herself. If that means that you are the source of the entertainment, so be it, but look to other ways to provide entertainment. You have a number of other things to do, not the least of which is making sure that you are taking care of your agreed upon role per the boss' instructions.

- Check with Boss…"Are things going OK?" If they aren't what can you do to help them get that way?

SERVING — DINNER

- Explain to guests the approach and gently nudge guests to seats or to the serving area, if it is a self-serve affair. Let people know it is time and what to do: ring the dinner bell.

- Beverages — more to everyone and/or inform them if there are different beverages being served with the meal.

- Verify that everyone is comfortable/served.

- Check with Boss…"Are things going OK?" If they aren't what can you do to help them get that way?

SERVING — DESSERT

- Repeat the steps above.

- Don't forget the beverages…suggestions:

o A re-fill of what your guests had earlier

o Coffee or tea (leaded and unleaded)

o Liquers or Wines

- Check with Boss…"Are things going OK?" If they aren't what can you do to help them get that way?

SOCIALIZING[2]

- Beverages…keep them hydrated

- Clearing…keep guest involvement to a minimum, unless you have insistent, enterprising guest(s)

- Check with Boss…"Are things going OK?" If they aren't what can you do to help them get that way?

WIND-DOWN/GOODBYE

- Verify the safety of over-imbibing of guests and either enlist taxis or designated drivers as needed.

- The Lingerers. This can be awkward, but there does come a time that you need to let them know that *the party's over*, and you should.

- Check with Boss…"Are YOU OK?" If she isn't, what can you do to help her get that way?

CLEAN-UP

- Try to leave as little as possible for the next day.

- Exclude guests unless, as with the clearing, you have some insistent guests that just have to help.

- Post Party Review (PPR) This is a great activity for clean-up. In some cases, it can be more entertaining for the hosts than the party itself. To truly execute this step, no one is protected and depending on how large a group you had and how much "fun" was had by your guests, the revelations discussed in the PPR can be hilarious. It is also a good time to discuss how you guys did as a team.

- Hug the Boss…she deserves it.

The key to a successful party is that both you and your guests enjoy themselves, and when I say "you" that refers to the plural you, including your wife.

I inserted the *check with the boss* item numerous times for a reason. The quick coordination "touch-base" is critical to covering everything that needs to be done, identifying any mid-course adjustments, and measuring how your wife is doing. I am not talking about scheduling a video call by checking calendars…I am talking about a quick verbal or non-verbal "everything ok?" If so, cool…if not, you catch it early and adjust.

> Note: As with most things, but most assuredly in the midst of a party, she is right. Deal with differences after everyone leaves, don't include your conflict as part of the party's entertainment. Trust me, your guests will enjoy it even less than you do.

As with that 7-iron or that Fly rod, the more you work on it and get the grooved swing or cast, the better it becomes. And we all have that favorite club/rod that when put in our hands we just know it will bring good things to the round/river. It didn't get that way overnight, it took practice. Have fun with throwing parties, mix it up and you will soon get a feel for what is most comfortable for you, your guests, and HER. You might even enjoy yourself. And more importantly, so will your wife!

HOW TO BE ARM CANDY IN 10 EASY LESSONS

Your wife deserves to be escorted by the best that the world has to offer. There are many definitions for the phrase Arm Candy. For our purposes here, I am referring the concept of how you can become the person whom your wife takes to any event that results in a positive reflection on her, either in a business or social setting. She already took the 1st step in selecting you to be her husband (and to be sure, while you probably popped the question, let's remember the person who was answering the question was in complete control of the situation).

The prerequisite to this lesson plan, is your agreement to actually escort her to business or social events. We could spend a lot of time on this, but I will simply ask you to look up the word "couple" in the dictionary, assume that you understand it, and proceed with my Top 10 Lessons to becoming Arm Candy.

- **Identity**…your overall objective in escorting your wife is pretty straightforward: **make her proud**.

And whose standard do we use to measure your success? Big surprise here....Hers. Here it doesn't matter if you are Clueless, Wannabe, Stud, or Romeo. I am not talking about the need to establish a "new you". She married the "old you" and if the pressures of work, peers, child-rearing, tax-paying, and sports-fanning have morphed you into someone else, it's time to think about regaining the cajones you had when you mustarded up the courage to pop the question and just be yourself.

One of the most difficult things to do in life is act like someone or something you are not. Further, unless you are a professional actor, you will invariably fail and the people that you are trying to fool will most likely view you as just that...a fool.

There is nothing more attractive and envied in social situations than the person, particularly a guy, who is genuine and comfortable. The only effective way to get there is to be yourself. You've got to be pretty special... that woman on your arm decided to marry you.

The remaining nine lessons are intended to polish that diamond that is the natural you.

• **Dress**...agree on proper dress, and the evening of, or right before an event is a little late to be discussing it.

Now if you are looking to make a style statement or you feel it is time to conduct a makeover, rev up the engines slowly, Mario and I would advise moving through the gears gradually. IF a big step is decided upon, involve her in the process. No deep dive here, there are many different ways to go and you can start that at anytime.

The key is to find something that fits you: physically, your personality, your social circles, and your wife's style. You are a team and while you obviously are going to wear different clothes (at least in public), it is important to complement each other and be consistent in terms of formality

If you care about how you look, others may or may not care. But it is almost guaranteed that if you _don't_ care, they will. And don't be disappointed if your attire is not noticed or acknowledged; the key is to remember that your appearance is a reflection on her.

Brief comment on shoes: if they had a shine when you bought them, make sure they have a shine now.

- **Posture**…Standing up straight sends a message to those that are observing — confidence. Slouches slouch.

- **Grooming**

    o **Hair**: Whatever style you have adopted for the thinning clump on top of your head , and wherever else it is growing, **neat** is usually identifiable and always desirable. Whether you have hair to your shoulders, the Trumpish comb-over (or whatever that thing is), none at all, and everything in between, a little thought a-**head** (sorry, couldn't resist) of the time that you will be escorting your wife is advisable.

    Most of us are always going somewhere with our wives. What does that tell you? Maybe attention to the mop on a scheduled basis is called for.

77

How often are the protrusions from the cranial follicles trimmed? Unless you are pulling off the retro mullet or the latter day hippie-shoulder length rock star looks, the rest of us can usually notice when you go beyond four weeks. The best way to measure how often you should get the trim? If everyone comments when you get it cut, you are waiting too long in between shearings.

Baby Boomer Alert! OK…let's be honest, as we have gotten older there are places that hair grows on our head that it didn't used to….ears, nose (inside and on top), brows, and that errant hair that just comes out of nowhere. And you are not alone if those errant hairs seem to appear and grow to a visible length overnight. With the exception of the well-groomed facial hair, it is a good idea to cut/trim the rest of it. Of course you can't do that unless you know it is there. And you won't know that it is there unless you look for it. Mirror, check. Tweezers, check…you are now ready for the weekly or bi-weekly discovery and extraction session.

Nasal hair is better smelled than seen. There really is nothing attractive about exhibiting your nostril hair and its filtering power. Moving up the face, unless you are making a fashion statement with braidable, Andy Rooney-like eyebrows, regular trimming there is a must….just keep it neat. Additionally, the ear hair is great for a dog, but unless your objective is to have someone come up and give you a good scratch, cut that crap off.

Mirrors may be required here, but for God's sake, take care of it.

- **Hands**…ok this is a touchy (pun intended) and personal area to which most men do not pay much attention. But beyond the handshake, your hands send a message that does warrant more attention than most of us give them.

Just as meticulous maintenance of sporting equipment or tools shows we're responsible and take care of things we value, a little attention to our fingernails shows we care. Pets should not get more nail attention than we do. So get ready: my suggestion is that you take the time to either provide yourself with a manicure-like grooming of your nails or get a manicure. Before you put this in there with my flower arranging suggestions, bear with me for a moment….At a minimum, your fingernails should be clean (top and under) and either clipped or filed neatly and evenly.

This can be a tough one for men whose occupation puts the appearance of their hands at risk. Additionally, certain medical conditions may keep some of us from being hand models. Regardless, to be Arm Candy, you need to take the time to do the best with what you have. Make the effort to "clean-up" and actually schedule the time to do it. In the same way you know how long it takes you to take of the three S's (Shower, Shave, and you know) in the morning, take the time to groom your hands. Result: Message to her, "Mmmmm, he cares." Message to new acquaintances, "She has someone that cares." If you are at a total loss on this, ask your wife to help you. Also, if you can muster up the courage, go into a nail salon and get a manicure. You may not want to do this regularly, but there is no better way to learn how to do the basics than to observe a professional – and you'll likely be surprised at the number of other men you see there.

•   **Conversation:** (n, an informal talk with somebody, in which opinions, ideas, feelings, or thoughts are shared) One key to being a good conversationalist is to take a genuine interest in what somebody else has to say. My wife is the best conversationalist I have ever seen, bar none. She can walk into a room of people she has never met and in 30 minutes have three new friends. And this is not just a one-time event, I have seen it time over time. At the core of her skill is her genuine interest in, and the entertainment she derives from, learning about other people.

Conversation involves the give and take of ideas and comments between people. Somebody once told me, "God gave you two ears and one mouth, and used in those proportions they will both serve you well." To be the sweet Arm Candy that you aspire to be, start out by being the facilitator of the conversation rather than the Lead Dog. Not that you shouldn't share your thoughts and ideas, but try to entice others to speak and you will find that the convo works better. And in most cases your spouse is more interesting than you are. (Personal note to my friends: I am acutely aware how much this applies to me.) So make sure that your wife is invited into the conversation; if she gets shut out, so will you (possibly in ways that are far more important than any cocktail conversation).

There are those among you who feel inadequate in social situations with your wife. You claim that you have nothing to talk about, nothing in common with the other guests, and just plain don't know what to say. You *non-conversationalists* can overcome this challenge through the recognition that there is one universal truth when it comes to conversation: Everyone is prepared to speak about and is expert on one subject — themselves. Further, most people want to talk about themselves more than anything else, don't you? The key here is to suppress the immediate desire to make it all about **you** and make it all about **them**. Once you get in the swing, the balanced sharing of **you** (opinions, ideas, feelings, or everyday topics) can kick in.

Open-ended questions, those that cannot be answered by a simple "Yes" or "No", are a very effective way to get things going. These questions usually start with "How...?", "Why....?", or "What....?". If you combine an open-ended question with the subject of the person with whom you are speaking, you are there. [1]

If you are naturally shy, you don't have to completely revamp your personality and become a chatterbox. In fact, not speaking and allowing others to carry the majority of a conversation, with a few interjections, is a great approach and can positively impact your ACQ (Arm Candy Quotient). Caution: These suggestions may actually lead you to learning, expanding your horizons, and being entertained, while at the same time thrilling your lovely wife.

---

1 *This works in conversation with your wife, as well, e.g. "How was your day?" (Don't cringe...you usually impose the incredibly impactful chronology of your day's experience on her, without her asking).*

• **Humor: OK, it's sensitivity time.** There are some among you that do not understand that what makes a joke or anecdote funny is that the person **hearing** it appreciates the humor, **not** the guy sharing it. If you are truly interested in conducting yourself in a way that makes your wife proud to be your wife, be very careful with the wit.

Most of us are just about the funniest people we know. We know this because the guys we work with and the people with whom we frequently socialize, laugh at our jokes. We know this because we appreciate the wide variety of humor that we are exposed to in everyday life, on television, in movies, email, the internet, etc, and in our estimation we are every bit as funny as those people in the various media.

The truth is we really aren't hilarious (rare exceptions) and not everything that is an attempt at humor is interpreted as humor by all people. There is a good chance that the people that laugh at your jokes have the same background and hold similar values as you. Then again, they may be laughing at your humor because they think that is the polite or politically appropriate thing to do. Has there ever been a funnier joke than the one the boss tells? Judged by the general response in a business meeting, no. You know the *over-laugh*. You've heard it and you've seen it. You may have even demonstrated it yourself. A classic example is the restaurant scene in *Goodfellas*, in which Joe Pesci's character is telling a story and Ray Liotta is splitting a gut laughing beyond the limits of what the humor warrants. Note: within 90 seconds he is also staring down the barrel of Pesci's gun. Me thinks there is a message there.

The fact of the matter is that unless you know people **very** well, you have no idea what their reaction is going to be to your attempts at humor. Therefore you need to be careful sharing that which you split a gut hearing for the 5th time, until you are certain of your audience. I say audience, because some jokes are overheard by people that are not part of the **intended** audience. Coupled with the social phenomenon that occurs amongst men in our society that the funnier a guy thinks he is, the louder he tells his jokes, the potential for offensive humor is actually pretty good. In a closed group, fine, in public, not so much.

What the hell does this have to do with your wife? Well Buck, if you have ever been on the bad end of the evil stare generated as a result of your inappropriate attempt at humor, you know. If you haven't, close your eyes and try to put yourself in the place of the character on the receiving end of Dirty Harry's, "Make my day." This is a situation to be avoided. The stare is just the precursor to the discussion/monologue/scolding that follows and remember, "Unhappy Wife…(Very) Unhappy Life."

Someone suggested to me years ago, that if you are ever trying to decide whether it is appropriate to share some humorous nugget in an unfamiliar environment, ask yourself if you would feel comfortable telling it to your mother. I have always understood that concept, even though some of the raunchier jokes I ever heard growing up were those that my mother picked up from the ladies at the beauty salon at which she was a client.

The point is: Tone it down. People's perceptions are their reality. To be social and to ensure that that woman to whom you are married is comfortable and proud of you in a social situation, save your Rodney Dangerfield-esque wit for the guys at the poker table.

• **The Introduction:** Pretty straightforward: Stand-up, smile, extend a hand and make sure you pick up the name. Repeat the name. If you have difficulty remembering names after someone is introduced to you for the first time, it is often either because you are too busy trying to rush to judgment on the person or are paying too much attention to what *you* want to say next. Slow down, smell the roses, live in the moment, and catch the name.

• **On Handshakes**: One of my Bucket List items is to share the following message with the Fish & Crusher grippers: Knock that crap off! My God, what is it with you guys?

I yield to the man with vice at the end of his forearm. OK, big guy, you are stronger…you win…now get over it and respect the long standing tradition of sharing a bonding moment by gripping and gently shaking another person's hand. Traumatizing the 27 bones and associated muscles, tendons, and ligaments of someone's hand, generates a reaction that is the opposite of what you are going for. And how big is your car? And how small is your…? Okay, I'll stop, if you will.

And to those of you that execute the handshake with the strength of a raw filet of sole, put a little effort into it. Unless your pathetic effort is the result of a debilitating muscle ailment, and my sincere apologies if it is, you are sending a message that you not only couldn't care less about the greeting, but that there could be something sinister and strange about you.....visions of Norman welcoming you to the Bates Motel, a la Hitchcock's *Psycho*, creep into mind.

Either extreme is troubling to the receiver. Get to the middle ground and stay. Good Dog!

When shaking the hand of a woman, let her dictate whether you are going to get a "manly grip" or you are going to get the palm down, "you should be kissing my hand, I am a lady, and don't forget it" hand shake. Either way, let her decide and respond appropriately by taking her hand and giving it a gentle grip.

• **Her Business Functions:** The key to pulling off the successful Spouse-to-be–Proud-Of maneuver is far easier than you would think. Keeping in mind the basic tenant of **your wife is always right**, look to her for guidance as to how to conduct yourself. Actually have the conversation to discuss what role she would like you to play. By the way, a conversation requires that the two of you stop what you are doing, make eye contact and conduct a dialogue on a specific subject. Reference your marriage vows.

If you have met the attendees at her function before, this may be a short conversation. But if this is your "coming out party", a review of the attendees, what their relationship is with your wife, and an understanding of what should and should not be discussed, can add to the success and enjoyment of the occasion. Depending on the degree to which your wife's work environment has a political element to it, you may also want to review people who you want to make sure that you socialize with and those that you should avoid.

I am not suggesting that you shouldn't be yourself, unless you are so socially unacceptable that you should only be allowed out of the clinic on weekends. I am just passing on some tips from my experience of being and observing the spouse at business events.

Also in the preparation file is the issue of attire. You want to fit in and not distinguish yourself by appearing to be out of place. As I have mentioned before, depending on the versatility of your wardrobe, having the discussion about attire 30 minutes before you need to leave for the event is analogous to a football team having their first discussion of how they are going to run the two-minute drill as they run out onto the field with 2 minutes on the clock and without ever having practiced it. Dressing should not be like drawing plays in the dirt at the playground. A little effort and preparation will not only make you more presentable, but make you feel more comfortable at the event.

Your wife wants people to be as impressed by you as she is. Little known fact: there is time set aside in every work schedule in American business for party reviews. This occurs over the few days following a party at work and involves the detailed review of every aspect of the party — the venue, the food, possibly entertainment, conversation, the host and hostess, and yes, Bubba, the spouses. There is an incredibly powerful impact associated with the receipt of a compliment about one's spouse. And you know it because you love it when your wife is the object of that compliment. Your sole purpose at a party is not to put on a show to get good marks. But recognizing the reflection on your wife and the positive impact your presence can have **is** worthy of your attention.

If business/social gatherings are not your cup of tea, don't attempt to compensate by making them your pint of beer. If you are prone to fall into the trap of wanting to have a few belts to calm yourself down and get "comfortable" with the situation, be very careful with this as what you may deem comfortable may be perceived differently. A social setting involving people with whom your wife works is not the time to convince one of her colleagues that 'you still got it" relative to your consumption of alcohol. It can also get embarrassing before you realize it, or your wife has a chance to rein you in. Moderation is the key here.

Regardless of the environment, keeping your wits about you is the most important thing. That way you will be able to maintain your judgment throughout the event.

And let's be honest, your wife would prefer that they see the person she married and is proud of, not your incredibly entertaining rendition of the Frat Boy Gone Wild (reference Will Ferrell's character, Frank the Tank, from *Old School*).

• **Your Business Functions**: Same as above. While in today's society, many families have both spouses working outside of the home, it is often the case that your careers have taken you in different directions and your work environment and co-workers are vastly different in job level, interests, and social demographics. Given that, it remains important that you return the same effort in preparing her for one of your business functions.

One of the more stressful situations at a party can be the introduction. Just as with her functions, it is essential that people engaging with you should be introduced to your wife. And it is helpful that if she doesn't know what they do, a brief description is appropriate, at the time of the introduction.

As dynamic as the work place is these days, even if your wife has been to many of you business-related events, it is important that you provide her with an update on people she has met before. Keep in mind that this person that you are bringing to the party — your date, your wife, YOUR Arm Candy — is special and the people she is going meet deserve to see her at her best. If she is walking into the situation blind, you run the risk of putting her into an uncomfortable situation — not good form.

Moreover, a social situation is a social situation and while work issues and conversation may get brought up, keep your wife engaged in the conversation, even if she is not participating verbally. If you have ever been in a situation in which two people get so focused on their conversation that they start to turn their backs on their spouses, you can see how isolated the spouse becomes. If it has ever happened to you, you can appreciate how awkward it made you feel. Be cognizant of the physical location of everyone in the conversation group and be inclusive.

When your wife comes to a professional event of yours, you are sharing the best part of you with your colleagues. The consideration you show her, and the strength of your relationship, can contribute positively to the image those associates have of you.

CHALLENGES ARE OPPORTUNITIES

SOME NEW PERSPECTIVES ON OLD – AND NEW – PROBLEMS

EMPLOYMENT'S NEW NORMS: TEAM CAREERS

The fact that recent economic conditions have not been positive serves to exacerbate the problem that not only is household income being stretched, but the stability of our job(s) is not what it once was. When second incomes were viewed as an extra, with the proceeds being used for toys, luxuries, or the basis for savings, the loss of a job could be weathered far more easily than today, when personal debt is up, net worth is generally down, and savings often non-existent.

Conditions like these tend to test even the strongest relationships and may also require a periodic redefinition of roles and responsibilities (as often as CNBC predicts the next recession, depression, market correction, or crash.) While these financial challenges are many, one constant these days is the importance of career decisions. And it is no longer just **your** call about just **your** career. We are now in the world of **Team Careers**.

More today than ever before in our history, our household financial state is the product of both husband and wife working outside the home. Whether this is result of necessity, convenience, or evolution, the fact is that when both of you are in the workplace, the variables in almost every area of your relationship just doubled. It is **not** just **one** schedule, **one** stress level, **one** political environment, (insert every aspect of your lives) and **one** income that needs to be understood, appreciated, and considered as you interact with one another. Because we want as much predictability and stability in our lives and finances as we can get, teaming with your wife on all things employment is key. And it doesn't matter if you both have a job, she works and you don't, or vice-versa, decisions need to be made as a team.

Nowadays we tend to define ourselves by the work we do and how much we make doing it. And this is pretty understandable with the number of us having to hold down multiple jobs, or putting the time into one that is almost equivalent to having another job. There is a saying in the hi-tech industry that you just have to work half-days....you get to choose which 12 hours. And a similar environment exists in other industries.

With the endless facets of our lives needing funding, much like hatchlings in the nest waiting for the parent to return with the results of his/her foraging for food, your occupation can become all-consuming. When considering a career change you need to expand your considerations and look at how the change impacts your life as a whole — and your relationship with you wife.

QUESTIONS

As you enter into the process of considering a job or career change or having one imposed upon you, i.e. lay-off, staff reduction; involuntary termination, limited restructuring, or any one of the variants used to describe your employer's act of letting you go, there is a significant amount of introspection required.

What are you best at? You should be looking at your skill set, your knowledge, and job related competencies.

What are your professional interests? You are served well by knowing what your preferences for positions, jobs, and companies are, as well as an understanding of what really motivates you.

What are your short- and long-term objectives? Having a vision of where you want to be and what you want to be doing is important, and in what timeframe. The application of your career's body of work and transferable skills to your objectives are also important considerations. You should also understand if there are skill gaps that must be closed to attain your objectives and how you plan to address them.

What are your Personal considerations? Your personal values, and how they align with your career plan, are critical. All of the considerations surrounding your family and work-life balance are often not given their due, but should be part of your list of considerations. And the two of you need to discuss if the change you are considering is realistic and feasible, not just something you are interested in and want to pursue. (A number of professional sources dealing with this topic can be found in the reference materials included at the end of the book.)

ANSWERS

There is a lot to think about here and the bigger the career step and the skill gap that you need to address, the longer it may take you to get to a stable situation. Further , the impact on your (meaning both you and your wife's) finances, lifestyle, and relationship is a primary consideration that you need to team-think with your wife. You both want you to be fulfilled, but at what price?

Why her? What better person to help you than the person who knows you better than anyone else? You may have a different persona at work, many of us do. But there is one person in the world who is most capable of cutting through your crap – your wife. She knows when you are truly passionate about something or just giving an academy award winning performance that may be impressing your current employer. Whose life, besides yours, is going to be impacted by the decisions you make? Your wife's. And on whose advice do you (or **should you**) rely on all other things? Your wife's.

Not that your wife is the only voice you should hear, but it should probably be the first and the last. And when was the last time she DIDN'T have the last word on something of importance? Crucial in this arena is your ability to effectively communicate the situation and solicit input. And while you may have very specific feelings or directions that you want to go, prepare yourself to answer the age-old question, "why?"

For a couple of reasons this may the most important aspect of your decisions relating to career and employment. First, once you know all the aspects of why, the what/where can get narrowed down very quickly. It also tends to distill the process into manageable parts. Secondly, your wife may live in this 'why" world more than you. And may be more expert in managing in this environment than you. Her vantage point is an essential complement to your own.

ROLE (RE) DEFINITION

Tradition and our view of traditional roles can work against our successfully examining our family situation and arriving at the "right" decision. Oftentimes, the view that we cavemen are the ones that must come back with the slayed carcass for the family blinds us to the reality of what truly is professionally fulfilling, personally satisfying and advantageous to the Team.

This works both ways in that we might not pursue our passion because we believe that we must be the primary earner in the family. Also, your wife may have an opportunity that if left to her own devices, would be financially and personally fulfilling, but we get in the way because "she can't do better than I." (I truly hope that most of you disagree with this observation and that it was a waste of space.)

Wake-up call, Lads: It's time to realize that there is no tradition worth following that should hinder your collective advancement — as a couple, a team, a partnership. I am not speaking about religious, holiday, or family traditions that deal with specific events or celebrations. I am referring to obsolete socio-economic traditions that you need to let go.

And, by the way, it is BOTH of you that need to let go. While we may feel that we are in an enlightened age of equality and gender neutrality, the concept of "women's lib" has not been adopted by all women. There's a fair number of women out there that still want to be "taken care of" and this may not be related to their earning power. It's just that their view of the world is influenced by their perspective on gender roles.

Clearing the mind to view our roles as team members may be a little more difficult than just saying, "OK...Done." It also involves the number of related roles (family, parenting, social, etc.) we may have established as a follow-on to the career paradigm. And if the "traditional" roles are the ones that are right for the Team....cool. It is just essential that a frank discussion take place and an approach is agreed upon for you to have a successful, joint go-forward strategy.

With all the considerations that may come into play in your process, it is important to remember the impact that the alternatives may have on your relationship. And not just financial and material considerations, but things such as travel and time commitments that may have a positive or negative impact on how you interact with one another and on your life together, should be part of your Team Think.

Regardless of how the two of you view your roles, the key is that you are open and honest with regard to what those are and how the two of you want to play the game. To **not** have a common view of each other's roles is a formula for frustration, mistakes, and potentially failure. Frank communication and agreement are not an option, but a necessity.

LISTENING

All of this is academic if we do not listen to one another and truly try to understand the situation from the other's perspective. Too often the conversation is treated like a post-game recap and analysis. Not good. Career and income issues are the big game and teamwork is mandatory.

QUICK HITS

Permission: As you start to engage your wife in this thought process, ask yourself another question, "Have I created an atmosphere in which she feels comfortable expressing her feelings openly and honestly to me?"

Honesty: As I mentioned earlier, one of the most important roles your wife may play is that of Cheerleader. And while pumping you up during the employment decision/selection process is incredibly helpful during the time, this is also a time when Honesty — I am talking **reality — tell it like it is — cut through the crap honesty** — is critical. You need to give her permission to suspend her duties as Ms. Ego Manager when it comes time for her input.

Handling Input: You have to be prepared to accept criticism that you may not be accustomed to hearing from her. No arguments, no disagreements, no qualifiers, just appreciation, acknowledgement of the help, and a kiss.

Input Killers:

- "I know, I know" (you probably don't)

- "Yeah ,Yeah" (So, now she's boring you?)

- Finishing her sentences (Did you really want any input on this?)

Clarifying:: When communicating your career plan and asking for input, the question, "Do you understand what I am saying?" is one of the more useless questions you can ask because the only response that will tell you anything is "No". The "Yes" response does not confirm that the person asked really understands, it just means they understand what they THINK you just said. Hint: ask them to play it back to you. I know this is Clarifying/Confirming 101, but if you listen to conversations you are a part of for a week, you will be amazed how rarely people truly confirm the understanding of what they have said and what they have just heard.

As with everything that is you, **you** need to make that final call, final evaluation, final sign-off on the plan that you are creating. That final call may not be 100% in sync with what you heard from her. But, Listen, Evaluate, Incorporate, and Appreciate her counsel in the spirit in which it was given. OK...stepping down from the Soap Box (for now)

Your Roles as Coaches

Coach (n. somebody who instructs a person in a particular subject or activity). Much of the previous discussion touched on the valuable resource that you and your wife provide to one another, that of being each other's Coach.

There are a variety of different approaches to coaching. Some are more aggressive than others. Some people naturally gravitate to a directive style, instructing the "student" on every detail of the activity. The other end of the spectrum is one that enables the student the opportunity to arrive at their course of action by asking questions or providing observations that may lead them in a direction.

When it comes to husbands and wives, understanding each other's interest in and style of coaching is essential to the effectiveness of the activity. The subject or object of the coaching activity has a lot to do with the approach that should be adopted and the way in which guidance will be received.

For this to work between you, have the discussion about how you want to work together. If the question doesn't get posed, prompt it. "I need you to provide some input to me in this area…." The boundary is important to identify because going beyond the agreed upon limits may negatively impact the understanding and acceptance of the input.

When I was in college, I was part of a major university's athletic program and was considering a career in coaching. In a conversation with the head football coach, he shared with me that the most challenging aspect of coaching is "knowing when to **stop** coaching. Knowing when to just rely on the fact that you have completed your work during the week and it's time to let them play." I suggest that knowing when it is time to let your wife "play", and vice-versa, may be the most vital aspect in your absorbing the guidance you have shared with one another.

That being said, providing guidance in a way that she appreciates and regarding subject areas in which you have expertise is key. I know you are the most intelligent person in the world and everyone comes to you for advice on everything. But in this case, admit there are limitations to your brilliance. You both need to know your limits, and with that knowledge you will both serve each other's interests well.

GAME TIME

Considering all of this does not make the challenge of career choices easier, but it helps ensure that the both of you are in sync and prepared for the future. Similar to the preparation of a team in a sporting event, the practice and creation of a game plan prior to the contest doesn't ensure victory, but in most cases it results in the team performing to its ability and maximizes the chances for success.

Get **your** team organized and prepared, establish your game plan, and enter the game with the best chance of winning.

WHO ASKED YOU? SHE DID! (HOW TO UNDERSTAND THE QUESTION AND ACE THE ANSWER)

Question. Questions. Questions.

Stimulus–Response...Yep.

Bell-Canine Salivation...Uh huh.

Cause — Effect... Got it.

Peanuts — Beer...Thank you.

Question — Answer...Gotcha!

Under normal circumstances A would follow B. But there is nothing *normal* about your lovely wife. I am not suggesting that she is *abnormal*. Let's just say **special**. And part of this specialness can be found in the dynamic that occurs when you hear that tone suggesting a query. Not all questions carry the fear as that bane of all questions "Honey?", referenced at the beginning of this guide. But it is critical that you pay attention to what is really being asked by your wife.

Were this any other person, you would take pride in the swiftness with which you accurately responded to the question…as well you should. But not unlike listening to a foreign language with which you have just a general familiarity, you need to take care in your response to your wife's inquisitiveness.

Clarity, not evasiveness, is the key here. And she knows the difference. In fact, the mere hint of evasiveness may not only discredit anything that follows, but be the genesis of a series of questions that may try your patience and sanity.

This is not to suggest a flaw in the female mentality. Just the opposite. It exemplifies two of the qualities that draw us to them in the first place: empathy and intuition. She knows when she is hearing the truth and has an appreciation for whatever the conditions are that might make that truth painful.

If Yogi Berra were to be a communications expert, he might let us know that, "50% of all communications is 90% nonverbal." And this goes double for her perception of your response to her (making it 180% nonverbal, Yogi?)

OK, Jim, so you're telling me that telling the truth is the right thing to do….well thanks for the tip. Fair—but I am really suggesting that first you know the motivation for the question so that you can answer the *real* question correctly.

You may feel that "hiding" irrelevant items protects your lovely from unnecessary detail and saves you from what you might feel is a highly inefficient conversation. But she may interpret your "managing" her through this process as your being disingenuous. You then run the risk of becoming guilty of a crime you never committed.

If, like me, the lady to whom you are married is brighter than you, (admit it), your managed answer may be suggesting that she is not quick or knowledgeable enough to grasp the REAL answer….."You want the truth? You can't handle the truth?!" (Thanks, Jack). Big Wrong.

The right answer to the question comes from the heart, only after you are sure of the question. And those people that told you it is improper to answer a question with a question are flat ass wrong. Clarifying a question by asking for further information is **entirely** appropriate and it enables both of you to get what you want.

One of the most common complaints of women with whom I have discussed this, is that they would like to be "heard" by their husbands. They don't just want us to sit there while we are being spoken to. Your wife wants to have what she says listened to and processed by you. The art of clarification is one of the best ways to not only truly understand what is being said, but to send her the message that she **is** being heard.

Is this over-think? Maybe. But if you have ever observed a presidential debate, or seen a business conversation in which the participants appear to be ships passing in the night, you know the value of clarity and honesty in the world of conversation. Jean Piaget, the Swiss Developmental Psychologist, in his Stages of Cognitive Development, speaks to this in the Preoperational Stage of child development, in which young children will be speaking to each other in sequence, totally oblivious as to what the other is saying. He refers to this kind of exchange as the "Collective Monologue." I think it is worth our time to rise above the habits of 5 year olds. Agree?[1]

And where is it more important to be effective in your communications than with the person with whom you are closest, the person who has your interest at heart, the person who is truly committed to your happiness?

As I mentioned earlier regarding arguments, lose them and fast. Actually, you should avoid them altogether by understanding the real question honestly and thoroughly, and responding accordingly.

THE MOTHER OF ALL QUESTIONS

My previous remarks notwithstanding, there are some questions that will come from the mouth of your wife that should resurrect a loop recording of the robot in the old TV series *Lost in Space*, "Danger! Danger, Will Robinson!"

"_____?" I leave that space blank, because I suspect you already had an example in mind the minute you completed reading the previous sentence.

---

http://www.telacommunications.com/nutshell/stages.htm

These questions fall into a few key categories and often start with the words, "Do you think that I look…..?" or the abbreviated version, "Do I….?" You may determine that there is a difference in these questions, one asking the absolute, one asking your opinion. Rest assured, they are the same. They are normally completed by references to physical appearance, change in physical appearance, or comparison of physical appearance to others. Sense a trend?

Variations involve the impact that clothing has on that physical appearance, e.g. . "Does this look……on me?" Do not be fooled, if it looks like a duck and walks like a duck….

The odds of guessing right when flipping a coin is 2 to 1; selecting the right number on a roulette table is a 38 to 1 proposition; an amateur golfer's odds of getting a hole-in-one is 12,500 to 1; and your chances of winning a state lottery range from 20-120 million to 1. However, if you want the best odds on earth, you can go to the bank that engaging in conversation with your wife on these questions is going to be trouble.

To be clear, there may a certain degree of sincerity in this request for evaluation, However, you are far more likely to be walking into a straightforward request for affirmation that you find her attractive. Your discomfort may not come from your response to the specific question, but the debate that often follows your response. Generally this is a no win situation.

This situation often precedes the impromptu fashion show in which you may have no interest in participating.

Advice…go with the fashion show, share your opinion on the most attractive outfit and avoid like hell the answer to the aforementioned questions. If these events precede the departure for a social occasion, you have significantly enhanced the odds of your enjoying the next few hours.

THE DAUGHTER OF ALL QUESTIONS

The "Why didn't you….?" question that is made in reference to the situation in which you were involved that did not end with the intended result. It relates to 20-20 hindsight, but is delivered in such a way that you are expected to reveal the failure of your perfect logic and well-thought-out approach to all things.

(Deep Breath…1…2…3) It is important here to avoid the primal urge to respond with "Because I am not as smart as you are, Einstein!" or some less eloquent variation. While that may be an accurate statement, the sarcasm with which you deliver it suggests you are trying to avoid the scrutiny and is a disaster waiting to happen.

Now there may be a number of circumstances that led you to the path you chose. Unless there is something to be learned by the analysis—something critically important—let it go, Buck. To debate the degree to which the intended result was not achieved is just plain stupid…reference earlier discussion of being Dead Right.

This is an excellent opportunity to respond with a clarifying question, and thus demonstrate your interest in being an experiential sponge, wanting to learn as much as she is willing to share, and your yearning to improve your future decision-making.

However, one of the best responses in this situation is to fess up. You are fallible. You certainly learned something from that one. You made a mistake, blew it, are not worthy; and are basically pond scum.

The Triple Threat

Last, but not least, is the trio of questions: "How could you...?" —-Why did you let me....?" —-Why didn't you keep me from....?" These questions are all related, often intertwined, and sometimes strung together. **"Why didn't you keep me from saying that? Why did you let me keep going? How could you just sit there and let me do that?"**

This triple threat of questions falls into a category I call the "expectantly rhetorical." This means that she may not expect an answer, but she sure as hell expects a reaction. With all of this said, as stated at the outset, let us never forget the Grande Dame of questions: "Honey?" But you already knew that.

This triple threat of questions falls into a category I call the "expectantly rhetorical." This means that she may not expect an answer, but she sure as hell expects a reaction.

You have a choice here, Chief. You can try to truly answer the question at face value, with practically no chance of recovery or wifely satisfaction, or you can think quickly and assume a sympathetic posture, acknowledging that you had indeed let her down in the situation. However difficult the latter may be, that challenge pales in comparison to the inevitably negative results awaiting you with the former.

With all of this said, as stated at the outset, let us never forget the Grande Dame of questions that we started this guide with: "Honey?" But you already knew that.

BEING A GOOD SPORT ABOUT SPORTS

ON YOUR INTEREST LEVELS

Sports and competitive athletics are an incredible source of entertainment, health, and learning. Personally, I have had the blessing of benefiting from all aspects of sports. They can also be a source of friction in relationships on multiple levels — usually when either the adult participant or spectator begins to take things just a little (a lot) too seriously.

Sports should be fun. When they stop being fun, it's time for re-evaluation. And how you approach sports can have a direct impact on your family and especially your wife. I'll touch on your role as the spectator role model in a little bit, but it is very important that your partner understands where you fall in the spectrum of sports interest, from casual observer to over-the-top fanatic...the variations are endless. And your personal positioning regarding your enthusiasm for sports is not always consistent with the rest of the "You" portfolio that your wife manages.

Once you graduate from your fantasy of actually making a living at your chosen sport, you need to create a balance with the other aspects of your life. The time you spend participating, spectating, studying to become more proficient at both of these needs to find a place that is in balance with all the other aspects of your life, not the least of which is the time and effort you put into the relationship with your wife. Now she may share in the pleasure of your various sporting accomplishment and your interest as a fan. In this case, you have the opportunity to kill two birds with one stone. This opens up terrific opportunities to stay close to one another.

However, when your collective interests are not completely in sync, you need to make sure that you don't take your eye off the real prize — **her**. You need to establish an understanding about the time commitment and expense of your other passion (name your sport) so as to not negatively impact your primary passion, **her**.

Some of you may have a bizarre notion that girls just don't get sports. In reality, your wife's ability to understand the nuances of sports and competition is just the same as yours…. it is a matter of choice, not cognitive ability.

To suggest that gender can impact the ability for a football fan to understand the nuances between a Cover-2 or Man-on-Man coverage; the success and expected result of a hockey team executing their break-out play; the mechanics and strategy associated with drafting in NASCAR races; or a soccer teams ability to create space and go to space, is ridiculous.

What is true, is that she may place a different importance on these than you do. Just because she may not want to get into a debate about a 3-4 vs. a 4-3 defense alignment in football, or whether the manager should have pulled the pitcher when he did, doesn't define her nor discount her. It may just indicate the degree to which she feels the subject is worthy of discussion. She may even adopt a manly approach to it, considering the results as the only important thing, and that to investigate the nuances and engaging in a debate of unattainable outcomes in the past, as a waste of time.

> "I have actually come to enjoy football…I just wish that the pre-game and post-game didn't last 6 days."
> Eileen, married 29 years.

Check it out and find the degree to which she aligns to your view of the sporting life and adjust your commitment to it. To be sure, there are plenty of marital situations in which both the husband and wife are equally enthused and involved in sports. I am suggesting that you understand the environment and loosen-up a little in the situations in which this is not the case.

YOUR KIDS' BIGGEST FAN

Over the years I, like many of you, have done my stint in volunteering to coach my kids' sports teams. Even if you haven't coached, you have probably attended a sporting event in which one of your children participated. In our efforts to support our children's efforts, we usually will shout out words of encouragement and support. While most the time he or she can't hear you, you do feel better for having sacrificed your voice, so shout it up!. The real value from your being the Fan is that you are there. That's it and that's HUGE. You are there, win or lose, achievement or failure, adulation or embarrassment.

But let's keep an eye on how enthusiastic you get and the impact that your going overboard has on your wife and the rest of your family. The expectations you have of a professional athlete, who is making millions of dollars and has spent years honing their talent to reach a level that entices you to spend significant money to watch them in person or commit the time to view them on television, is appropriately high. My question is, what did your 7 year old do to deserve the same treatment?

LIGHTEN UP, BUBBA!

Take a couple of spare hours and go to a youth sporting event with which you have no connection….baseball, softball, soccer, it doesn't matter. Sit off to the side and observe the various styles of parental conduct and get ready for some astounding behavior. I know, you've seen it all…been there — done that. Humor me (and yourself) with this one. There is something about being completely removed from involvement with the kids, the teams, the coaches, and the parents, that provides this activity with a strong return on investment.

The spectators are all out there with varied motivations. For some, it's the socializing with the other parents. For others, it is the most important event of their lives, with their futures being inextricably tied to the skill their child demonstrates or the success their child's team enjoys in the event. Others are physically there, but mentally checked out, demonstrating that they are the most important people in the world as they focus on their PDAs.

But you will see him. He is always there. Sometimes he has a buddy, but often he is the Lone Wolf. He may be the smartest man in the world....knows it all. (He may not be a **he**, but this is a guy's guide). He knows more than the coaches, the other parents, and the officials. And he lives to let everyone know about it, regardless of the negative impact he has on not only those people, but most importantly the kids.

You will also get the chance to see the kind of "I am so embarrassed for you" moments that you get watching Lucille Ball in a rerun of an *I Love Lucy* episode, or Steve Carell in *The Office*.

And the offenders seem oblivious to the impact of their actions on their wife and kids. It is as though the entrance into the sports environment releases them from any obligation to conduct themselves in an acceptable manner, by anyone's standard.

I may be describing you and you don't know it. If your wife is of the same disposition, she may not know it either. If she isn't, do yourself (and your kids) a favor and ask her, with assurances that you will actually listen to the response and not argue the validity of her observation and/or conclusions. Listen, learn, and change, if appropriate.[1]

And since we are there, when you do express your very lofty expectations of the professional athlete, either in person at the event or at home, take note of your environment before you decide to embark on your scatological outburst, however well-meaning or humorous. Remember my comments about humor in public? They apply here. I have been a season-ticket holder for a major sports team for over 20 years....I have heard some classic lines...some hilarious, some obscene. The line should be drawn when the conduct serves to only demonstrate the limits of your vocabulary and desire to be a negative example to the younger set. If only you had the video camera and could see yourself.... You'd change.

I am not talking about loud, enthusiastic positive support. That's really hard to overdo. I am talking about the negative comment, the berating of officials, the verbal evaluation of a child's performance, etc. Truth is, you may not be qualified to even evaluate them (officials or kids), the impact on the child notwithstanding…**It's Lighten Up Time!**

The value of competitive athletics for kids is derived from their learning a little about the sport, their experience in teaming with their peers, physical exercise, and in most cases, establishing a relationship with an authority figure outside of the family. There is also a benefit of having the family share in that development and joining in the FUN of it all. Winning? Scoring? Statistics? Give me a f*#@ing break.

Once in a great while there is a truly gifted athlete that comes from these environments. And yes, certain appropriate steps should be taken to develop that rare potential. But, all of the aforementioned are still part of the development package.

My observation of literally hundreds of soccer matches, hockey games, and swim meets has led me to a conclusion: there is a inverse correlation between a parent's own athletic accomplishment and their predisposition to engage in this aberrant behavior. Not that all wannabe jocks act like asses, but if you see the behavior, there is a good chance that someone is trying to rework their athletic history, living vicariously though their children. If I just described you, please consider the following: it is their time. Let's support it, not try to live it for them.

AND WHILE WE'RE AT IT.....

The legendary football coach, Vince Lombardi was quoted as saying "Winning isn't everything, it is the only thing.." And while many a misled jock may follow this quotation, according to the late James Michener's *Sports in America*, Lombardi claimed to have been misquoted. What he intended to say was "Winning isn't everything. The will to win is the only thing." [1]

The difference between the intent and application of these two quotes is at the core of the difference between true sportsmen and the misled, and often insecure, sports fanatics. Actually, that which is learned from failure is usually far greater than the lessons that are remembered from victory, but both are important. My suggestion is that if you are involved in amateur athletics, as an organizer, coach, parent, or participant, you spend as much time on the available learning opportunities as on the drive to win.

End of sermonette. Now go out there and tell your 10 year old to go kick the others team's ass! **Not!**

(Michener, James A - Sports in America. Fawcett Crest, 1987. ISBN 0-449-21450-8) .(http://en.wikipedia.org/wiki/Winning_isn't_everything;_it's_the_only_thing#cite_ref-Michener_3-0)

THE STRENGTH OF YOUR
WEAKEST MOMENTS

On the somewhat serious side of masculinity, in our society there is this concept that to show that you have been emotionally impacted by something is a weakness. I am not talking about your expression of jubilation toward a victorious team or athlete — that is consistent with the stereotype. I am talking about that thing, anything, that truly touches you and, if you allow it to, takes you where you may not go very often. It could be a song, a scene in a movie, or a personal event in your life.

Have your eyes ever misted up watching a movie? Have you felt that tingle observing your kids achieve a goal? Or have you experienced an event in which you felt pride in your wife's achievement? Felt that pain from the loss of a loved one? If so, did you try to hide it, or let it out and let it show?

Somewhere down the line, you may have received a message that you were supposed to stay cool and staid in the face of such events. If ever there was a time to "shoot the messenger", that was it. I wish we could rewind and replay that tape differently.

That the expression of sadness, disappointment, pride, or jubilation in response to a personal loss or success is a weakness, is complete BS. To the contrary, I would suggest that the inability to feel and further, express, those emotions is a flaw. **It is the soft spots in your heart that define a significant part of who you are.**

While both ends of the spectrum may have been stifled, it's likely that the response to the negative has been more suppressed than that to the positive. And I am going to dive into that murky pool here. When faced with a family loss or major illness, it is often considered the role of the man to be the rock, the stability, the one that everyone can rely upon for strength. And while you may assume that role, especially for your wife, it does not mean that you must be void of all expression of emotion. On the contrary, your expression of emotion, your demonstration that there is a soft spot in your heart around a sad event, is a **showing of strength.**

THE EMOTIONAL ROLE MODEL

Throughout most of this book I have avoided the specifics of child-rearing and the impact that it has on your married life. This was done intentionally, not in any way to diminish its importance, but to try to keep our focus on the lady with whom you are teaming to bring up those rug rats. I do however want to bring up one point here that relates to you as a role model — for your wife and your kids.

Regardless of the persona that you have as the DAD and HUBBY, the lack of expressing emotion is not going to do anyone any good at all. To see that their hero is devoid of emotion can lead those in your fan club to be under the impression that suppressing one's emotions is to be admired. After 50-something years of observing and personally experiencing this approach, I submit that the opposite is true. You, me, all of us, need to help break the vicious cycle.

Among all the many cues on how to act that *those* people look to you for, there are two that are pretty damn important: how to love and how to endure a disappointment or loss. This guide deals predominately with the expression of love for your wife. But I would also challenge you to give your fans the opportunity to develop their own personal way of processing events and experiencing emotions by allowing them to see that it is OK to hurt and grieve: my Dad/my Husband *feels* things. If this concept strikes you as self-evident, excellent and thanks for your patience. If this concept seems new, different, unimportant, or out of place, spend a little time to think through it. Me thinks that those around you (and you) will benefit from the investment.

Give me a minute to step down from the soap box (again)…. thanks.

DEALING IS NOT JUST FOR CARDS

Life must go on and the journey continues despite the changes in the plan. Professional golfers do not intend to hit their ball into the rough, but when they do, they immediately re-evaluate their position on the course and make a new plan for their next shot; they adapt to the current circumstance. While many of my fellow golf fanatics/addicts can draw parallels between the game and life, one area where the parallels do fail is this: unlike in golf, where you may, in a matter of minutes, adapt to your new norm, when faced with life-changing tragedies or personal losses, many people do not/ cannot /and should not be expected to adapt that quickly.

The old adage "time heals all" is true only as long as people get what they need to heal. The part you may be required to play in the process is varied and may change given the circumstances of the event. This applies when you are the caregiver / supporter, as well as, when it's you who needs these things. You are probably used to adapting quickly. In many cases this can help you, but applying your adaptive techniques to some situations can be counterproductive, especially when you need to go through the grieving process and take the time to heal.

With respect to your wife, just being there, *on her terms*, is probably the most important role you can ever play. This may mean providing a shoulder, a hug, a gentle or strong hand to hold, or a handkerchief. It may also mean providing space, covering some duties that allow her to have downtime, or simply listening.

Being there for you. And oh by the way, if you take a look in there where you may not usually go — inside where you **do** feel, where doubts and unanswerable questions reside — you may find once in a while that **you** are in need of the same things.

She is probably holding back and waiting for you to ask for support. Unless you have shown this side of yourself to her, she may not be sure what you need or how to engage. This is where that previously referenced role of managing your ego can create a little complication. If she perceives that you think it is a weakness to be emotionally hurt, she may avoid asking or acting. So it's time to man-up and ask — asking for emotional support, in whatever form you need it, is not a weakness! In fact, it may be seen as appealing and attractive.

This isn't intended to be a ploy. What I am suggesting is that your genuine expression of needs, beyond those of the typical culinary and carnal variety with which she is oh so familiar, is manly, an expression of strength, and something that will most assuredly be met with a positive reaction.

Your ability to be in touch with your emotions is huge. But to do this you have to allow yourself to **feel** them. I could go into a lot of detail about the ways in which we are so adept at blocking our emotions and feelings and the variety of ways in which we anesthetize ourselves…leading to abuse issues, and all that comes with them…but I am not going there. Suffice to say (and repeat) that to be in touch with your feelings, you have to allow yourself the opportunity to actually **FEEL,** and to do that you need to have a clear head and body chemistry.

Final thought on Dealing. As I suggested earlier, adaptability is one of your strengths, but holding others to your standard can be dangerous. There are certainly societal and religious traditions on dealing with serious health issues and death. Beyond those guidelines, there is one thing that I have learned as a result of having gone through a number of these situations: EVERYONE needs to be afforded the ability to handle things/grieve in their own way.

There are books that go into the various predictable stages

of grief and I am not suggesting to rewrite the theories and studies by those learned women and men. Regardless of the approach with which you identify, religiously or scientifically-based, very simply, people need to be provided the freedom to deal with things in the way that feels right for them.

Some will want help, professional and non-professional alike. Some will want to do it on their own. Some will desire solitude to cope, others will have a need to **not** be alone.

Whatever the personal choices, and most especially those made by your wife, the path through the grieving process is always best decorated by your support of those going through it in a way of **their** choosing.

Whew! Where did we go there, Jimbo? Just a little trip into the world that exists outside of all the fun and games, joy and happiness, the two of you share. It is essential that your "vulnerable strength" pop in there when needed, to strengthen the bond you have with that one person....your loving wife.

MANLINESS DOES NOT EQUAL CAVEMAN-LINESS

There are a few things that are purely masculine...and not too many of those are all that pleasant...except to us. In this section I am going to share a few of these characteristics/ situations with an eye on their mitigation, to the extent that they could be a source of friction with Her.

ON FONDNESS OF FLATULENCE

Flatulence (noun): excessive gas flatus in the digestive system

Fart (noun): The release of intestinal gases through the anus, usually with an accompanying sound...from the Middle English word "ferten" meaning to break wind.

While this act of breaking wind is very natural and common it is also considered unacceptable and vulgar to perform in public. And that is why none of us have ever done it in *public.*

It is important that I clarify that this issue is truly critical to the male existence and involves a rather complex concept of two dimensional planes (the Manly Dimension and the Womanly Dimension), co-existing in such a way that they should never meet. For should these two realities lose their distinction, the repercussions would be of epic proportions. For the Trekkies in the crowd, this is analogous to the coming together of matter and anti-matter…not a good thing.

The Manly Dimension: The Manly Plane of Existence is that world in which men exist either alone or with others and in the absence of women. Here the act of breaking wind is as accepted as other physical occurrences or environmental phenomena. In this reality, every quality of the event is sensed, evaluated, enjoyed, and compared. Scent, tonal quality, duration, personal pleasure, and in some cases, causality are all considered when the event occurs. In this world, attribution is never projected to one's pet or other people and its ownership is often held in high esteem by he who created the event and sometimes by witnesses, as well. The event itself has _risen_ to such a level of acceptability as to have innumerable names, verbs, and phrases created to describe it.

In this world, even when some aspect of the act is viewed as unpleasing, public evaluation or commentary is usually accompanied by a smile and possibly a humorous comment. It is considered a natural occurrence for which there is no negative impact to either the individual, their immediate audience, nor the environment, in general. It just **IS**.

The Womanly Dimension: This existence is defined as being in the presence of any female within olfactory or audible range of the potential creator of the flatulence. In this environment, men strictly observe the long held tradition of not breaking wind, lest we draw the ire of our mates. There is a logic to this. Most women will claim that they have rarely actually experienced such an event caused by a woman and certainly never been the creator.

While attempts are made to suppress certain qualities, such as the noise, associated with a standard fart, all evidence of the event cannot be concealed. It is for this reason, that men must strictly adhere to the guiding principle of the Womanly Dimension: it is a "No Fart Zone."

A curious characteristic of this dimension is the predisposition and active production of flatulence by household pets. The frequency and strength of flatulence from pets in this dimension is significantly increased, particularly in comparison to their presence in the Manly Dimension.

Adherence to the Womanly Dimension's guidelines by all men, is responsible for the eradication of almost all arguments and discord involving flatulence in our society and has been widely applauded by women, the world over.

> "The last time I was at my sister's house, my bro-in-law, who I have known since I was six, let one rip. We'd all been silently drinking coffee and reading the morning paper, and all looked up in shock (no awe.) "Robert!" my sister exclaimed. I guess he had finally become too comfortable around me." — Marie, too long an in-law

On Manly Dexterity
(with sincere apologies to Shakespeare)

To pick or not to pick, that is the question:
Whether 'tis better to withhold the urge
To satisfy the itch from every source and manner

Or to take finger against one's bodily complaint.
And by scratching end them? To rub, to scratch the itch,
And by a itch, we suggest
The inflammation, and the million irritants
That we as men must bear: 'tis a condition
Strongly to be endured. To rub, to scratch the itch;
Perchance the crotch- ay, there's the rub:
For in that joining of leg and trunk, the satisfaction
From either front or back yielding matchless pleasure.

When from this mortal existence we do finally depart
Who among us may, nay, would desire
To claim ignorance of one's nasal or otological spaces?
Or to have not digitally remove matter lodged 'tween one's teeth?

O to survive this conundrum of propriety of action,
Bearing heavily upon our tenuous survival upon this spinning
orb.

This guilty pleasure, this rude gratification,
Unconsciously defining our gender's weak resolve.
To be of two minds, two worlds, two planes
At what price? Would one even ask if energy and awareness,
were the legal tender required to satisfy the instinct?

To wit, never shall you survive in the absence of such necessities,
Yet the performance of such may best be done sans audience.
As with all things personal, decorum is in the eye of the beholder....

The true measure of man's magnitude being seen through that lens.
The tolerability of these endeavors fully comprehended
Would dictate the degree of public display.

With consciousness on high, could needs co-exist with etiquette?
Per chance, vulgarity share space with proper comportment?
Should the search for temporary privacy be too high a price,
To be at once boorish, fulfilled, masculine, and acceptable?
To say not is to be in accord with thine consort
And to exist in both manly and marital bliss.

Abrupt Segue Alert: From the highly personal activity to the place where these kinds of activities should occur.

ON ETIQUETTE D' BATHROOM

As you faintly hear the harsh tones of Axl Rose, screeching "Welcome to the Jungle," it is time that we acknowledge that there is a space in your residence that is plain and simple, HERS! Regardless of its dimensions or functionality, your status within the bathroom(s) of your home is that of a second class citizen.

Further, questions from you to your wife regarding activities that take place in Her bathroom, must be considered long and hard before they are asked. I was asked by an executive early in my business career, "Do you know why the Sperm Whale has the smallest throat of any whale?" I responded, "No." To which he said, "I don't know why either, but that's the way it is!" The business context of the conversation led to a discussion of how to recognize when certain business circumstances are not changeable or the endless conversation concerning alternatives has come to an end. Its application here is that we need to really think before posing the question,

"Why do you (anything) ?" with respect to the bathroom. The most appropriate explanation when it comes to her activities in the Room is, "Because that's the way it is." It's a Sperm Whale, my friend.

The exception to this caution can be found in the reason for asking the question. If the answer is truly going to be heard by you, processed, and result in you understanding of something that you **really** wanted to understand, then go for it.

Questions in this area can, in some cases, lead to a positive reaction from your wife. For instance, if you have ever taken the time to observe your wife's preparation regimen in the bathroom, you will likely observe a series of planned, well-orchestrated activities. These involve the use of a variety of appliances, instruments, products, and procedures, all brought into play in precisely the correct way and time as to result in the work of art that is the lovely creature to whom you are married. If you don't have an immediate appreciation for the process, think of it as a very long auto-racing pit stop, sans the tires and gas.

The intricacies and nuances of the process and the skill employed to complete the tasks are many and detailed. If you REALLY want to understand the process then ask your questions. She will appreciate your interest and you will gain an understanding of how essential each step is in the process.

However, if on the other hand, your objective is to lead her to what in your mind is an easier, more expeditious approach, well Ahab, your time would be better spent pursuing the whale. I'm not advocating the need for separate facilities or the elimination of substantive health/hygiene discussions between you and your wife. What I am saying is that her activities in the bathroom have been genetically encoded over generations and are not likely to be influenced by you, regardless of the substance or merit of your inquiry or suggestion.

Further, the priority which she holds for the use of the facilities is unfortunately for you, out of bounds—-the term "ladies first" was actually originated with respect to her priority in the bathroom and THEN extended to the application to the order of passing through a doorway and escaping from a sinking ship.

I know, I know, didn't I just suggest that you need to spend more effort on your own appearance? Didn't some of the suggestions create a demand for a little more time in the "personal prep hall"? Well first of all, kudos for remembering. And while you will indeed need to spend a little more time, do not expect the new-found attention to your appearance to take precedence over hers. After all, you need to remember, It's All About Her. As I shared before, her processes are well-honed and predictable. It may be time to employ your highly-developed negotiation and planning skills in mapping out when each of you will need to use the facilities.

Even if you are fortunate enough to have a more spacious bathroom with a couple of sinks, this coordination may still be required. You are well aware of this if you have ever made the mistake of taking a shower as your wife is finishing her hair preparation and been held responsible for the destructive effect that the resultant steam has on your wife's "do". Been there? You know. Not been there? Trust me, it ain't a fun place.

In summary, it is her domain and you are guest. The satisfaction of your experience is entirely up to you, but always under her control.

BLAME IT ON THE BOSSA NOVA

You are a logical, prescriptive man who is able to find the root cause or at least justification for just about everything that occurs in the natural world. Further, you may also have started to develop your Bucket List, that list of things that you aspire to accomplish prior to "kicking the bucket". However, your ability to fulfill that list is directly tied to your acknowledgment of the following: there are a number of things, some of which I will relate here, for which you are to blame. Some of these are a stretch and some with which you totally disagree, but the reality is that you **are** to blame. So, I submit to you

THE BLAME LIST
(Abridged with tongue firmly lodged in cheek)

• The toilet seat being left up

• Fluctuation in shower temperature… regardless of your proximity to the local toilet

• Her being late in preparing for any social outing

• Smudges on her recently painted finger/toenails

• Her not having "anything to wear" (Solvable…see earlier chapter)

• Appliance, child, and pet events' impact on her preparedness for anything

• Her receipt of a traffic ticket

• Her failure to renew a driver's license

• Her luggage being overweight

Manliness Does Not Equal Caveman-liness

- Childbirth labor being painful

- Her having overslept

- Her being Late (yeah THAT late)

- Her forgetting what she was gong to say

- Her computer crashing

- Her computer crashing without having a recent back-up

- Her having a non-flattering picture taken of her

- Her having taken a blurry picture of a one-time event

- Her gas gauge being on E

- Her inability to find her glasses, her keys, her anything

- Her running out of hot water

- Your failure to properly relay a message for Her

- The Pets having fleas

- Bad service at a restaurant

- The inadequacy of any hotel room

- Any negative conduct of your children

- Her over-cooking a dish

- Her under-cooking a dish

- Her breaking of a dish (or anything else)

- A bad table location at a busy restaurant

- Her bad hair days

- Bad weather at an outdoor social event

- Her over-embibing

- The Sun rising in the East, setting in the West, and there being only 24 hours in the day.

- And lastly, any situation in which she is wrong, because…she is always right…and that's about it, Forrest.

WRAP-UP:

LIFE AFTER DRINKING THE KOOL-AID

Dara's Top 10

MY GREATEST HITS (AND PERHAPS YOURS)

After consulting with my best friend, I have compiled a few of her favorites...a few of the occasions that I have been successful in throwing a little more fun into the game. And again, money is not the key to pulling this off; over half of these require no cash. This is mano y mano with no personal agenda, other than to create a little spark in you, Romeo. Enjoy.

The Chauffer: My wife was out of town and expected me to pick her up by driving up to baggage claim at the airport. I decided to dress in a black suit, white shirt, black tie, arrived at the airport early, met her as she came out of the secure area as her Limo Driver with a sign with her name on it from "Fantasy Transportation" "We Pick you Up and Hook you Up"...a good evening.

The Card: One Valentine's Day I became the Valentine's Day Card...Pretty straight forward: with Red Marker I printed

Be My Valentine on my chest...lots of opportunity for creativity here (before and after the card is read)...a very good evening.

The Letter: Finances were tight one year and we agreed that what money we did have, we would spend on the kids. I wrote her a love letter, put it in an envelope; put the envelope into a box; and wrapped the box as I would a Christmas present....a good Christmas.

The Gown: Last year I took my lovely out to select a dress for our son's holiday season wedding. I decided to splurge and purchased at a high-end store. After the dress selection, while she was picking out shoes, I communicated with the shopper that a beautiful gown, not appropriate for the wedding, but perfect for an upcoming New Year's Eve Party, should also be added to our selections. When she went for her fitting for the wedding dress, she was also surprised to find out that she was also having the second dress fitted. She was the belle of the ball.....a good New Year.

The Stroll: One Valentine's Day our gift to each other was a stroll across the Golden Gate Bridge. For those of you familiar with San Francisco in February, it is a "bundle up and hold each other to stay warm" kind of walk. Half way across, I gave her a little gold locket with a picture of the two of us.....a good day.

The Masseuse: We had both been having a rough stretch at work and personal life and needed some serious help to chill out. I had met this masseuse at a golf tournament and she shared with me that she would be willing to come to our home and give us each massages...stop that thought now...I am talking a professional here and not that profession. 2 hours each on the table she set up in our bedroom to candlelight and recorded nature sounds. Incredible. Thanks Jenn!...a verrrrrrrrry relaxing evening.

The Stars: Not a one-time event.... on a summer evening, under the stars on the chaise lounges listening to the music from the iPod. A little wine, could have sworn a few UFO's, a little conversation, and a little hand holding…a nice evening

The Gifts: On a 6 day trip to St. John, I packed greeting cards for each morning and evening, and a gift to start every day that was loosely related to the activities planned for that day. Nothing expensive, just fun. Added a little mystery as to what each card would relate and how many ways I appreciated her. ….a great week

The Song: Another repeat event. Whenever we go into a bar or restaurant that has somebody playing music, I secretly find my way to the musician and ask him/her to play "our song", in our case, *Your Song*…a little tip and I'm set. Memories about how it became our song and the times and places we've heard it come back….great memories

The Present: After having figured out how to side-step our *rule* for not exchanging gifts for our 10ᵗʰ anniversary, I called ahead in the early afternoon to the restaurant where we were to dine that evening. Our friends at Bridges (in addition to be a great place to dine, it is notable for having been the location for the dinner scene in *Mrs. Doubtfire*) were very accommodating by having the bracelet I had wrapped as a gift, delivered with our cocktails…..nice Anniversary.

The Painting: Maybe my best…my darling wife loves pictures and paintings of doors. In addition to the composition itself, the story and opportunity that may exist behind the door fascinates her. We have purchased a number of tropical and Mediterranean pieces from an artist in Hawaii that we both enjoyed and have displayed in our home. For a Christmas present a few years ago, I commissioned the artist to paint the front door to our home from photos I provided him. His oil, entitled "Dora's Home" was a hit. Thanks, Mike Carroll!.... nice Christmas

The Book: Well, if you haven't figured it out yet, this book, like all things, is All About Her…thank you, Baby……Great Wife!

….and a damn good life.

YOU CAN DO IT

If you have gotten this far, you probably realize that I have drawn you into reading a How-To book that was outside of your usual interest. Millions are spent on home maintenance manuals, DVDs to improve your golf swing, and tips on how to ensure the perfectly green lawn and full blooms. But it is not very often that men spend the time doing the same investigation into treating their wives well and thinking about how to make their relationships more enjoyable.

I do not have all the answers and do not imply that my suggestions are applicable to all situations. Further, my intent is not to pass judgment on you or your relationship with your wife. Hell, you're married and that is some heavy lifting in and of itself. My only hope is just that you consider different ways to make your relationship with your wife a little more respectful, romantic, and fun.

As I have shared these ideas with colleagues and friends over the last few months, there have been 3 common responses, alone and in combination with one another:

 # 1. The real or virtual "Kick under the table from the wife" reaction. This may be disguised as an emphatic glare sending the "See?!" message to her husband; the "Wow, wouldn't that be that be nice?!" delivered with a high level of sarcasm; the casual, yet meaningful punch in the arm; and any number of variants that add up to the "It's time to step up, Pal" message.

#2. The "Thanks Jimbo for screwing it up for me and the rest of the guys from the husband" reaction. This will usually be preceded by some obscenity and involve significant rolling of the eyes. Accompanied by an expression of disappointment and amazement that some guy actually went to the trouble and took the time to write all this stuff down, this reaction conveys the frustration that his wife's expectations have just been raised….unsaid, "Damn, more work!"

#3. The "You actually share your reactions to this guide and take the opportunity to touch base with one another and do a check-in on your relationship" reaction.

My sincere hope and original intent in sharing all of this with you was that the **Discussion behind Door #3** would occur.

Early in this book, I suggested that your wife is always right and that you should abdicate control to her. Here is a major, if obvious, exception: take full control of the one area for which there is no doubt of your ownership…..how you show her that you care for her, you need her, you desire her, and you love her every [expletive deleted] day of your lives!

If as you read through the guide, you picked up something that you can use or found yourself engaging in conversation with your wife about what makes her happy; less stressed; more desired; or simply, more loved...**mission accomplished!**

Now how does all this relate to Winning the War? There isn't any "war" unless you make it one. If you adopt a position of respect, fun, and romance, the time you would have spent developing your strategies and plotting your tactics, are spent on far more exciting and pleasurable pursuits.

As unpredictable as you may consider your wife to be, the appreciation shown in response to a little caring and an "it's all about her" attitude, is usually shown in the return of the favor. As with most things in life, your relationship runs more smoothly when there is balance. Give-Take, Ying-Yang, Ali-Frazier, Magic-Bird, Jack-Arnie, Phil-Tiger, er… maybe the last one is not a good example for this purpose, but I think you get the idea. .

My experience is that our lives are pretty structured and we often seek time to escape the stress and demands placed on us by our workplace or social circles. It is also my experience that when the relationship with your wife is based on a few basic niceties, you are afforded the ability to pursue your personal escapes and are actually encouraged to do so.

At the end of the day, it is the emotional bond and love between you that matters — all that I have shared with you is intended to awaken these.

While some of the activities and perspectives that I have suggested may have previously appeared to you to be God-awful, I encourage you to keep an open-mind. I know that the two of you heading off to the spa together for joint his/hers massages may seem to be the most ridiculous vision you could ever have. But get prepared, one of the likely consequences of engaging in some of these activities is that there may be a new definition to what you view as enjoyable, relaxing, and fun.

More importantly, you may end up getting to know that woman you married a little better and realize that you Won the War, way back when she said "Yes."

ACKNOWLEDGEMENTS

- To Herb Caen for your wit and "…"
- To Mark Twain and Henry Chaucer for your timeless writing and humor
- To William Shakespeare for the art of words
- To every patient English teacher that attempted to learn me how to right
- To every person with no respect for the English language for providing the example of how it should not be used
- To Cindy Kanegis for your coaching and support
- To Ken Traylor for your artistry, illustrations, and patience
- To Usher for seeing my vision
- To Yvette Bozzini, my editor extraordinaire, for helping not only get it done and get it right, but for enabling everyone to know what I really meant to say.
- To the JUGs for asking for it
- To Buddy for always agreeing with my ideas
- To Alexa for being my hero
- To Tom for always being there
- And last but never least, to Dora…it truly is All About You!

BIBLIOGRAPHY/REFERENCE MATERIALS

Bibliography

- Shakespeare (reference to Hamlet's soliloquy)
- Maslow ((Abraham Maslow[citation needed
- Piaget (Santrock, John W. (2004). Life-Span Development (9th Ed.). Boston, MA: McGraw-Hill College - Chapter 8)

Reference Materials

o Perspectives

- Don't Sweat the Small Stuff in Love by Richard & Kristine Carlson http://www.dontsweat.com/
- When Bad things Happen to Good People by Harold S. Kushner
- The Happiness Project: Or, Why I Spent a Year Trying to Sing in the Morning, Clean My Closets, Fight Right, Read Aristotle, and Generally Have More Fun by Gretchen Rubin

o Ordering Flowers

- 1800Flowers.com http://ww32.1800flowers.com/
- Teleflora http://www.teleflora.com/
- FTD http://www.ftd.com/

o Language of Flowers

- The Language of Flowers – Wikipedia http://en.wikipedia.org/wiki/Language_of_flowers

o Women's Fashion

- The Style Checklist: The Ultimate Wardrobe Essentials for You by Lloyd Boston

- The One Hundred: A Guide to the Pieces Every Stylish Woman Must Own by Nina Garcia

- I Love Your Style: How to Define and Refine Your Personal Style by Amanda Brooks

o Courtesy and Etiquette

- Real Men Belch Downwind: Modern *Etiquette* for the Primitive *Man* by Mike Nichols

- Look, Speak, & Behave for Men: Expert Advice on Image, Etiquette, and Effective Communication for the Professional by Jamie L. Yasko-Mangum

- Essential Manners for Men: what to do, when to do it, and why by Peter Post

o Party Planning

- The Party Planner: An Expert Organizing Guide for Entertaining by Kimberly Schlegel Whitman

- Simple Stunning Parties at Home: Recipes, Ideas, and Inspirations for Creative Entertaining by Karen Bussen

- Do It for Less! Parties: Tricks of the Trade from Professional Caterers' Kitchens by Martha Hopkins

o Men's Style and Grooming

- The Art of Manliness – Website http://artofmanliness.com/category/dress-grooming/

- Valet – Website - http://valetmag.com/

• How To Be a Man: A Guide To Style and Behavior For The Modern Gentleman by Glenn O'Brien and Jean-Philippe Delhomme

• Esquire The Handbook of Style: A Man's Guide to Looking Good by The Editors of Esquire Magazine (Editor)

o Conversation Skills

• How to Win Friends & Influence People by Dale Carnegie

• The Fine Art of Small Talk by Debra Fine

• The Pocket Guide to Making Successful Small Talk : How to Talk to Anyone Anytime Anywhere About Anything by Bernardo J Carducci

o Massage Techniques

• The Book of Massage: The Complete Step-by-Step Guide To Eastern And Western Techniques by Lucinda Lidell

• Treat Each Other to a Rubdown—Article in Women's Health http://www.womenshealthmag.com/sex-and-relationships/ sensual-massage#axzz1mCw4GuHW

o Vacation Planning

• Fodor's Travel Intelligence — Website http://www.fodors. com/

o Spa Guides

• About.com Spas – Website – http://spas.about.com/

• Spa Finder – Website http://www.spafinder.com/

• Destination Spa Vacations http://www.destinationspagroup. com/

o Bed & Breakfast Guides

- The Innkeeper Bed and Breakfast Guide http://www.theinnkeeper.com/

- Pamela Lanier's Travel Guide Books by Pamela Lanier http://www.lanierbb.com/bookstore/bookstore.html

o Mike Carroll's Gallery

- Mike Carroll's Lanai's Fine Art http://www.mikecarrollgallery.com/

o Career Planning/Counseling

- 1010 Tips for Successful Career Planning by Randall S. Hansen, Ph.D. http://www.quintcareers.com/career_planning_tips.html

- Taking Charge of Your Career Direction: Career Planning Guide, Book 1 by Robert D. Lock

- Career Match: Connecting Who You Are with What You'll Love to Do by Shoya Zichy with Ann Bidou

- What Color is Your Parachute? By Richard Bolles.

- How to Find Your Mission In Life by Richard Bolles.

- Creating You & Co: Learn to Think Like the CEO of Your Own Career by William Bridges.

- Do What You Are: Discover the Perfect Career for You Through the Secrets of Personality Type by Paul D. Tieger and Barbara Barron-Tieger.

- The Power of Purpose: Creating Meaning in Your Life and Work by Richard J. Leider.

- Who's Running Your Career? by Caela Ferran.

Made in the USA
Charleston, SC
02 February 2013